The Politics and Strategy of the Second World War
edited by Noble Frankland and Christopher Dowling

FINLAND 1939-1940

D0848933

ANTHONY F. UPTON

FINLAND
1939-1940

NEWARK
University of Delaware Press

FIRST AMERICAN EDITION PUBLISHED 1979

Associated University Presses, Inc.
Cranbury, New Jersey 08512

Library of Congress Catalogue Card Number: 79-52235
ISBN 0-87413-156-1

PRINTED IN THE UNITED STATES OF AMERICA

CONTENTS

MAPS

EDITORS' INTRODUCTION

Numerous books have been written about the battles and campaigns of the Second World War and the flood of new titles shows no sign of diminishing. Yet, though the fighting has been described in detail at a tactical level, the reasons why the various campaigns were undertaken remain comparatively obscure. The aim of this series is to examine the background to some of the more significant campaigns and to assess their impact on the course and outcome of the war as a whole.

To what extent were the disparate strategies pursued by Britain, France and Belgium responsible for the overwhelming defeat of the Allied armies in 1940? Was the German invasion of Russia an ideological indulgence or a military necessity? Did it render British strategy in the Middle East irrelevant? Could a different sense of priorities have saved Singapore in 1942?

These are among the questions which the series will attempt to answer. Although nearly thirty years have passed since the Second World War ended we are still living in its shadow. The war transformed the political and social structure of almost every belligerent power. By uncovering the motive forces which lay behind this cataclysmic conflict the series will, it is hoped, help us to understand how the post-war world came to be forged.

NOBLE FRANKLAND
CHRISTOPHER DOWLING

I

The Background to the Crisis of 1939

In 1939 Finnish independence was scarcely twenty-one years old: from 1809 to 1917 Finland had been part of the Russian empire, in which it had the status of an autonomous grand duchy. For the first ninety years of this connection, although there was a Russian governor general and Russian garrisons in the country, Finland's internal autonomy was respected and there was no serious friction between the Finns and their Russian overlords. But in the 1890s Russian governments had sought to increase control by methods which infringed the legal and constitutional rights of Finland. This in turn provoked bitter resistance from Finnish nationalists, who led a campaign of patriotic resistance to Russian imperialism. In this period of conflict, between 1899 and 1917, when the Finnish leaders who were to direct policy after 1917 were coming to maturity, the idea took root that Russia was the implacable enemy of the Finnish nation and would always seek its complete subjugation. The consequences of the Russian revolution of 1917 were superimposed on this background: the Bolshevik government had recognized the independence of Finland at the end of December 1917, at a time when there were still large numbers of revolutionary-minded Russian soldiers and sailors in the country. When, in January 1918, the Finnish socialists proclaimed a workers' government in Finland and tried to overthrow the new bourgeois republic, a bitter civil war broke out. In this war the Russian government and its troops in Finland gave arms and assistance to the Reds, while the Finnish Whites got aid from Sweden and Germany. The Reds were defeated and savagely repressed, while their leaders fled to Russia and there founded the Finnish Communist party.

During the Russian civil war the Finnish government

had supported the efforts of the Germans, the British navy and White Russian elements to destroy the Bolshevik régime, sometimes allowing operations to be mounted from Finnish territory. Although Finland and Soviet Russia had signed a peace treaty in 1920 at Tartu, and correct diplomatic relations were established, there was no mutual trust, and Stalin was to reveal in 1939 the deep impression these events had had on his thinking. Furthermore, the Finnish government had, from the beginning, treated the Finnish communists as traitors and tools of Russian imperialism. The support which the communists received from the Soviet government, through the Comintern, was held to prove that at some time the Soviet Union would try to reverse the verdict of 1918 and use the Finnish communists to bring Finland back under Russian control. Given this historical background, the Finnish leaders found it difficult to believe that Russia would seek genuinely peaceful and friendly relations between Finland and the Soviet Union. It was a natural reaction when former president Relander wrote in 1934 that 'as long as the Soviet Union supports the revolutionary aspirations of world communism . . . its peace propaganda is to be treated with reserve,' and for the foreign minister, Hackzell, to write to the ambassador in Moscow in 1935 that the poor relations between Russia and Finland must be regarded as normal and that no improvement was looked for.[1]

Ideological conflict was one cause of distrust: in addition there were old-fashioned considerations based on military strategy and power politics. The geo-political significance of Finland in northern Europe was considerable and diverse. The Finnish west coast, and her possessions of the Åland islands, gave her a dominant position in the Gulf of Bothnia; on the one hand the Åland islands dominated the sea approaches to Stockholm, and on the other Finland was in a position to control the route along which Swedish iron-ore was shipped to

[1] K. Korhonen, *Suomi neuvostodiplomatiassa* . . ., II, pp. 48, 72. (Hereafter *Korhonen*).

central Europe. It was true that the Åland islands were demilitarised under an international convention of 1921, but this only meant that they were open to seizure by an unscrupulous or desperate great power and that Finland had little prospect of defending them. Thus in this direction Finland was of the greatest importance for the security of Sweden and for the war-making capacity of Germany, which depended on imports of Swedish iron-ore. In the far north, the Finnish province of Petsamo divided the Soviet Union from Norway and direct access to the Atlantic ocean, while the Finnish border was a bare hundred kilometres from Murmansk, the only ice-free Russian port on the open ocean. In addition the area had proved to contain one of Europe's richest deposits of nickel, a vital and scarce strategic metal: the concession for exploiting this belonged to a British-Canadian company and consequently the Soviet Union for strategic reasons, and Britain and Germany for economic reasons, were keenly interested in Petsamo.

The long eastern border of Finland flanked the important Murmansk railway, which linked that port with Leningrad and the interior of Russia. The unique position of Murmansk among Russian ports meant that the railway was regarded as a major strategic factor both by Russia and by her potential enemies. In addition, Finnish nationalists had long dreamed of incorporating the province of Eastern Karelia, through which the railway ran, into an independent Finland, for it was partly inhabited by Karelians, who spoke a language closely related to Finnish and who were regarded by the nationalists as a lost tribe of the greater Finnish nation. In 1919 and again in 1922 expeditions had been launched from Finland aimed at raising the issue of secession among the Karelians; and the continuing aspirations of the Finish nationalists to secure this *terra irredenta* were in no way concealed. No one in Russia could suppose that after 1922 the Finns by themselves would attempt a forward move into this region, but it was clearly possible that a hostile power seeking to enlist Finnish support against the Soviet Union would offer the possession of Eastern Karelia as a powerful inducement for Finnish cooperation.

But the supreme strategic importance of Finland lay in her southern coast. From Hanko eastwards the steamer channels to Leningrad were dominated by this coast and its archipelago, and by the islands in the Gulf of Finland belonging to Finland. In theory, whoever controlled this coast could block the Gulf of Finland and all sea access to Leningrad (the second city and only Baltic port of the Soviet Union), especially since the fortifications put up by the Tsarist governments for this very purpose still remained intact in Finnish control. Then on the Karelian isthmus, the Finnish frontier at its closest point was a mere thirty-two kilometres from Leningrad, and well within heavy artillery range of the city and of the naval base of Kronstadt. The dangers to Leningrad were obvious and had been noted by the Russian negotiators during the peace conference of 1920. The Russians had declared that the independence of Finland meant that Leningrad 'has now got into a quite impossible situation' and that 'if we start from the point of view of strategic defence, then the Russian government would of course be obliged to demand in the most stringent fashion that not only should the islands in the Gulf of Finland be joined to Russia, but also a considerable portion of Finnish territory along the coast towards Viipuri'.[2] This is interesting because it anticipates very closely the position that Stalin was to adopt in 1939, and suggests that demands for the revision of the settlement of 1920 along these lines was inherent in the situation which the peace treaty had created. Clearly the use or possession of southern Finland by an enemy of Russia would be a deadly danger to the safety of Leningrad, and gave ample reason for the Soviet government, its friends and enemies to be seriously interested in the area.

Yet Finland, with all its geo-political potential, was

[2] K. Lehmus, *Talonpoika suurten shakkilaudalla*, pp. 14, 22. (Hereafter *Lehmus*).

inhabited by a nation that numbered a bare three and a half million people between the wars – in population one of the smallest independent states in Europe. Nobody could imagine that the Finns by themselves were a threat to anyone's security, for the strategic potential of their country could not be exploited by them, but only by an outside power. However, it was precisely for this reason that, although the Finns threatened nobody, they were always the objects of the hopes and fears of other powers who would not allow Finland to enjoy the isolation from international conflicts that most of her people would have wished. That was why Finland was a problem for the leaders of the Soviet Union. It has been shown that they had grounds, based on their historical experiences in the civil war period, for assuming that the Finnish government was fundamentally hostile to them and that it would not be averse to allowing powers hostile to Russia to use Finnish territory for their attacks. The assumption was valid in one respect – the Finnish government was basically unfriendly to the Soviet Union – but it was unsound in the conclusion to be drawn from this: nobody of importance in Finland contemplated allowing a third power to use Finnish territory for an attack on Russia. Finnish thinking was defensive and started from the premise that Russia had its own imperialist intentions to undermine Finland's independence. This thinking was typified by former president Svinhufvud in a series of talks he had with German leaders in 1937. Svinhufvud supposed that strategic considerations alone meant that Russia must seek to recover her old dominance over Finland, and hence there could never be really friendly relations between Finland and Russia. The Soviet Union would always be Finland's enemy and the enemies of the Soviet Union Finland's friends.[3]

The evidence suggests that the Russian leaders held fairly consistently to their interpretation of Finnish intentions. Up to 1933 they were sure that it was the British imperialists who were preparing to attack them

[3] *Korhonen*, p. 74.

through Finland, after 1933 it was the Germans – yet in both cases they were wrong. The British, after their unhappy attempts at intervention in the Baltic immediately after 1918, had lost all serious military interest in the area, and their activity there was purely commercial. While Hitler, among his many plans, had no designs on the countries north of the Baltic, it was the consistent aim of German policy to keep Norway, Sweden and Finland neutral in the event of a European war so that the Baltic would remain an open sea for Germany, and the resources and raw materials of the area would be freely available for the German economy. This was one direction in which Hitler genuinely had no territorial ambitions. This situation enshrined a classical and self-fulfilling recipe for disaster. Because one of the Russian assumptions was obviously correct, and the Finns made little attempt to conceal this, it was supposed that the other assumption, which seemed to be its logical concomitant, must also be true, and it was on this false basis that the Soviet government framed its policies. Naturally, all Finnish attempts to prove the falseness of the second assumption were treated as deceptions.

This situation prevailed in Finnish-Russian relations until 1936, although it was true that in 1932 a non-aggression pact was concluded between them and was extended in 1934, but no mutual trust developed from this. Soviet commentators noticed that many people in Finland openly welcomed the revival of German military power under Hitler, that Finland was officially unenthusiastic about the Russian entry into the League of Nations in 1934 and that unofficially the event caused demonstrations of protest in Helsinki. Trade between the two countries, which was trivial at the best of times, was stopped altogether by the Russians in 1934. In 1936 Russian military commentators claimed that the capacity of Finnish airfields far exceeded any forseeable domestic needs and was clearly designed for use by other powers. Yet by this point the Finnish political leadership had come alive to the dangers of their position, and in

December 1935 the government announced a major policy change designed to create a more tolerable situation – this was the announcement that henceforth Finland was definitely aligned with the Scandinavian neutrals, and that this would be the basis of her future policy.[4]

The immediate Russian reaction showed the same mixture of correct observation and false deduction: the Russians noticed that Germany favoured Scandinavian neutrality and had therefore welcomed the Finnish move. It followed that there must be ulterior motives involved and that Finland was to act as a link bringing the Scandinavian neutrals into line with German policies. The Russians were encouraged in this interpretation because some people in Finland did see the move in this light, and saw Finland's role as preventing the neutrals getting involved in the Soviet Union's attempt to form a front against the aggressor states. But the Finnish government had genuinely hoped that strict neutrality would offer Finland a way out of her involuntary involvement in great power conflict. The Russians gave no credit to this at all: as late as October 1937 *Pravda* characterized Scandinavian neutrality as really helping the aggressor states. In November 1936, Zhdanov, the new boss of the Leningrad party machine, had made an ominous speech in which he declared that his city was the object of fascist designs and warned the small neighbouring countries that 'it does not pay small countries to get entangled in big adventures.' He went on to say that if they did lend themselves to the plans of the aggressors, 'then we shall feel compelled to open wide our windows facing them and with the help of the Red Army have a look at what is happening.' This was generally taken to be a warning to these countries, of which Finland was clearly one, that if they lent themselves to German designs, Russia might be compelled to launch a pre-emptive move into their territory – an interpretation which was shown to be correct

[4] *Korhonen*, pp. 82, 96, 113, 126, 132: T. M. Kivimäki, *Suomalaisen politiikon muistelmat*, pp. 93-5.

during the talks with the British and French governments in 1939.[5]

Thus Finland's new policy of alignment with the Scandinavian neutrals did her no good at all in the eyes of the Soviet Union. In November 1936 the Finnish ambassador in Moscow warned his government that Russia had no confidence in their professions of neutrality and that urgent corrective action was needed if relations were to improve. The chance came after the general elections in Finland in 1936, followed by a presidential election early in 1937, had brought a more progressive government to power. The new foreign minister, R. Holsti, was an outspoken critic of Nazi Germany and made the improvement of relations with Russia his first priority. Holsti offered to make an official visit to Moscow and the offer was accepted at once. He had talks with Litvinov, Voroshilov and other Russian leaders, who told him that an improvement of relations was possible but that Finland must give some concrete assurances that her neutrality was genuine: this meant realistic undertakings to prevent the use of Finnish territory by third powers for an attack on the Soviet Union. The outside world took the visit seriously, the Russians relaxed their propaganda against Finland, while the German leaders, especially Göring, voiced anger and concern. This was echoed by the Finnish Right, which attacked Holsti for senselessly alienating a sure friend in pursuit of a chimerical notion of collaboration with the Soviet Union. The critics need not have feared. Neither Holsti nor his government colleagues had any intention of offering the sort of pledges that the Russian leaders were looking for – and without such pledges suspicion was undiminished on the Soviet side. The visit of a German naval squadron to Helsinki in 1937 was very unfavourably noticed in the Russian press and treated as backsliding. When a strong German delegation came to Finland in 1938 for the twentieth anniversary celebrations of the White victory in the civil war, a similarly adverse interpreta-

[5] *Korhonen*, pp. 134, 135.

tion was put upon it. The Soviet press once more took up the theme that Scandinavian neutrality was in effect pro-German, and that in the case of Finland it was evidently fraudulent. However, behind the façade of propaganda the Soviet government did begin a prolonged testing of Finnish intentions, which led straight up to the crisis of 1939. This was connected with a major shift in the line of Russian foreign policy, which became apparent early in 1938: the idea of collective security through the League of Nations was virtually dropped – Litvinov said as much to the American ambassador in March. Instead the Soviet Union prepared to deal with the German danger either by a direct bargain with Hitler, or by a straightforward alliance with Hitler's opponents, combined with a strengthening of defences towards the west. In April 1938, B. Jartsev, officially only a second secretary at the Russian embassy in Helsinki, but in fact a direct representative of the highest levels of the Russian government, began a series of strictly secret talks with Finnish leaders. He said that the Soviet government knew for certain that Germany planned to invade Russia through Finland, and added that Finland could prove her intentions by agreeing to let the Soviet Union help her repel such an attack.[6]

As a result of these conversations, which were known only to a handful of leading politicians in Finland, the positions of the two sides had crystallized by August 1938. The Finns wanted Russian recognition of their Scandinavian neutrality policy, which had acquired a new substance in July 1938 when Sweden and Finland agreed in principle on joint plans for the defence of the Åland islands. The Soviet government was wholly opposed to this scheme, which it characterized as German-inspired, noting Germany's undisguised approval of it. The Finnish leaders then offered Jartsev a bargain. They would give a firm declaration of intent that Finland would resist any attempt to use her territory for an attack on Russia,

[6] *Korhonen*, pp. 152-3, 159, 160: M. Jakobson, *The Diplomacy of the Winter War*, p. 14. (Hereafter *Jakobson*).

and in return the Soviet Union should drop its opposition to the plans for defending Åland. The Russian counter-proposal was that Finland should reinforce a declaration by stating her willingness to accept Russian assistance in repelling an attack; Finland by herself might fortify the Åland islands provided Russia was allowed to keep observers there; and Finland was to permit the establishment of Russian base facilities on the island of Suursaari in the Gulf of Finland. Finally, as a further inducement, Russia was ready to offer Finland an advantageous trade agreement. The Finns refused even to discuss such proposals; they would not enter into any agreement involving active military cooperation, actual or potential, with the Soviet Union on the grounds that this would be inconsistent with true neutrality. Although exchanges of view continued sporadically after August, the deadlock was complete. In December 1938 Mikoyan told a Finnish delegation in Moscow that while the Soviet Union accepted as genuine the desire of Finland to be neutral, it could not believe that Finland by herself could maintain her integrity against an outside intrusion into her territory. There must be concrete guarantees of an effective defence.[7]

By that time the Finns were less impressed. They read the Munich crisis as a sign of Russian weakness and isolation; their ambassador in Moscow reported that the Soviet Union could scarcely be ranked with the great powers and the Finnish government thus felt both safe and justified in remaining totally unresponsive to Russian approaches. In February-March 1939 Russia made a last effort at direct negotiation through a new emissary, B. Stein, who came to Helsinki with a fresh proposal. Instead of a base on Suursaari, which could be held to compromise Finnish neutrality, the Soviet Union would lease, or exchange for territory elsewhere, the string of lesser islands in the Gulf of Finland which covered the sea approach to Leningrad. This time the Finnish leaders

[7] *Jakobson*, pp. 41-6: V. Tanner, *The Winter War*, pp. 3-13. (Hereafter *Tanner*).

consulted their chief military adviser, Marshal C. G. Mannerheim, who urged them at least to enter into negotiations, and not send the Russian away empty-handed, for he took the realistic view that a small power like Finland could not afford to return an absolute refusal to a great power in pursuit of its security. But the Finnish ministers were unmoved; they refused to discuss the new proposals and Stein went away in April remarking that the Soviet Union could not credit neutrality without guarantees and would renew its proposals. In fact the Russians seem to have concluded that their worst suspicions were true – Finland was implacably hostile and in league with Germany. Maisky, the ambasador in London, said as much to the British government, while the new Russian foreign minister, Molotov, in his only conversation with the Finnish ambassador prior to the outbreak of the European war, concluded that 'the behaviour of the Finns shows that in Finland they are trying in every way to strain relations with Russia.'[8]

The Russians were correct in supposing that it was no use talking with the Finns, though they misread the reason for this. They assumed that Finnish indifference to their approaches was based on encouragement from Germany. In fact it rested on a serious underestimation of Russia's power and determination, combined, paradoxically, with the suspicion that any Russian proposals must conceal some ulterior design against Finland's independence. Thus when Germany did offer to conclude non-aggression pacts with the Scandinavian countries in April 1939, Finland joined Norway and Sweden in refusing. They meant to demonstrate the immaculate nature of their neutrality. The Russians had decided to get what they wanted over Finland's head, either through negotiations with Britain and France, or through a bargain with Germany, but in either case they would demand a free hand in Finland. In the abortive negotiations with the western powers they were induced to agree, in spite of vigorous Finnish remonstrances, that if Finland

[8] *Korhonen*, pp. 179, 195: *Jakobson*, pp. 62-5: *Tanner*, pp. 14-5.

were to become the object of German aggression, or voluntarily lent herself to Germany's designs, then the Soviet Union would be entitled to move in to her territory and repel the danger. But in the end it was the alternative bargain with Germany that was realised, in August 1939, and the secret protocol to the German-Soviet pact, which defined the mutual spheres of interest, put Finland in the Russian sphere – the Finns of course did not know this, but their fate had been sealed.

During this same period the Russians had also been making plans of a different kind. At the end of 1938 the Leningrad military district began an urgent review of its military preparedness, which was in part a reaction to the unyielding attitude of the Finns in the diplomatic negotiations. Russian accounts confirm that these preparations simply assumed that Finland would be a willing collaborator in any imperialist attack on the Soviet Union. The defensive plans were overhauled, and in particular big improvements were made in the communication and supply facilities along the eastern border of Finland with Karelia. In June 1939, Stalin summoned a conference on Finland which included general Meretskov, commander of the Leningrad military district, and the exiled Finnish communist leader, O. W. Kuusinen. The conference assessed the political situation and Stalin expressed his conviction that either of the imperialist camps might use Finland as a base for hostile operations. There was evidence that the Finns had made extensive advance preparation for this, and Stalin claimed that intelligence showed a major development of base facilities in Finland. If Germany were the aggressor then there was no doubt that she would come through Finnish territory. Meretskov was ordered to draw up contingency plans to meet the danger. These were reviewed at a further conference with Stalin and Voroshilov in July and were based on the assumption that the Leningrad military district must handle the situation out of its own resources. Stalin, who had characterized the danger from Finland as 'alarming', exercised close personal supervision over the preparations. Meretskov's memoirs, which do not specify the exact nature of the plans, speak of a 'counter blow' as their central feature, and it seems reasonable to conclude that in the event of war the Russians were planning to move into Finland and meet the enemy threat there. This is in fact what Voroshilov told the Anglo-French military mission in August 1939 was the basis of the Russian war plans.

On the Finnish side there had been no equivalent military preparation. They had redrafted their military procurement programme in 1938, but the basis of this was to rely increasingly on the domestic manufacture of arms, rather than their importation. This meant that in 1939 the programme was still at an early stage of development because the necessary plant had to be developed and licences sought for the foreign weapons they wished to make. The target date for completion of the programme was 1944, so no sense of urgency was shown, and the results of this leisurely approach to the problem is demonstrated by the fact that thirty Vickers tanks, purchased in 1936, still had no guns in 1939. Outside Finnish government circles there was alarm at the growing international tension, and right-wing political leaders and patriotic organizations financed a volunteer movement for people to spend their summer holidays of 1939 working at fortifications on the Karelian isthmus. The government, though unconvinced of the urgency of this, gave official consent for the work to proceed in April 1939. Even the German-Soviet pact failed to shake the complacency of the Finnish government; indeed, they interpreted it as reassuring, on the grounds that if there was no longer any danger of conflict between Russia and Germany, neither power could have any reaon for objecting to Finland's neutrality. Nor did the outbreak of European war in September seem to give any immediate cause for alarm in Finland, which joined the other Scandinavian countries in declaring neutrality. On 17 September, when Russia collected the first instalment of what was due under the German-Soviet pact by moving into Poland, the Finnish ambassador was assured that as far as his country was concerned the Soviet Union was completely neutral and that the Russian government was confident that Finnish-Russian relations would improve, indeed there was some sign of renewed progress in the long drawn out negotiations for a trade agreement. When the Finnish foreign minister talked to the German ambassador on 20 September he was in a most optimistic mood, and anticipated new political discussions with the Soviet Union in which Finland might consider offering to cede the lesser islands in the Gulf of Finland in return for Russian approval of the Finnish-Swedish plan for the joint defence of Åland.[9]

Then, on 25 September, the illusion began to crumble. On that day Stalin told the German ambassador in Moscow that he was going to solve the problem of the Baltic states, though he did not mention Finland. That same day Estonia was presented with demands for a mutual assistance pact which would allow Russian bases to be established in the country, the Estonians submitted, and Latvia and Lithuania were compelled to follow suit within a few days. It was not difficult to guess what would come next, and those Finnish leaders who knew about the secret talks in 1938-39 believed that they could anticipate what line the Russians were likely to take. On 5 October Molotov presented a note to the Finnish ambassador requesting that the foreign minister should come to Moscow to discuss 'concrete political questions'. For Finland, the moment of truth had arrived.[10]

[9] K. A. Meretskov, *Na sluzhbe naroda*, pp. 177-9. (Hereafter *Meretskov*): *Jakobson*, pp. 90-2.
[10] *Jakobson*, p. 101: *Tanner*, p. 19: *Documents on German Foreign Policy 1918-1945*, Series D, VIII, p. 106. (Hereafter *DGFP*).

II

From Diplomacy to War, October-November 1939

The Finnish government had not waited for an actual demand before taking action. They had read the signs aright on 25 September and did the obvious thing – to find out what the German attitude was. On 26 September foreign minister Erkko told the German ambassador that Finland would never accept the kind of terms that had been presented to Estonia: 'Finland will never submit to a Baltic solution . . . we would rather let it come to the worst.' This was the first of a series of probes designed to stimulate German support for Finnish resistance to the Russian demands. The ambassador in Berlin made approaches on 2 and 9 October, and on 6 October Erkko asked the German ambassador outright for his government's support. At the same time the German embassy in Helsinki was flooded with calls from prominent Finns seeking assurances of Germany's help. But this activity was all in vain; the German-Soviet pact meant that Germany had renounced the right to intervene in any way between Finland and Russia, and Hitler had no possible motive for endangering the fruits of the pact in order to help Finland out of its mess. The German foreign office drafted a memorandum on 7 October defining the official attitude: Germany would not interfere in any way in questions between Finland and the Soviet Union and would advise the Finnish government to accept whatever terms were offered. This same advice was repeated by Göring in reply to various Finnish enquiries and by Hitler himself to the Swede, Sven Hedin, on 16 October – Hitler was confident that Finland would yield to necessity and come to terms rather than fight a hopeless war. There is evidence that even the Nazi government felt mildly uncomfortable in taking this attitude, for there was a strong residual pro-Finnish sentiment in Germany derived from memories of 1918, and it flourished at the highest levels of the military and bureaucratic establishment. Von Ribbentrop, for instance, had to tell the ambassador to stop a proposed visit by former president Svinhufvud to canvass German support, since it would be utterly futile and could only cause needless embarrassment. This attitude of the German government on the Finnish question never deviated throughout the subsequent events, and on more than one occasion Hitler personally intervened to insist that it be adhered to. Thus the only great power which was in a position to act effectively on Finland's behalf refused to do so.[1]

The Finns had meant it when they said that they would not submit to the kind of settlement imposed on the Baltic states, and as a result they took their time before responding to the Russian invitation to talks. In the meantime, on 6 October, they mobilized the field army and followed this up on 10 October by calling out the reservists, which amounted to general mobilization. They further decided not to send the foreign minister to Moscow, but instead made the ambassador in Stockholm, J. K. Paasikivi, their representative. Paasikivi was beyond question a good choice. He was a conservative banker, who could never be suspected in Finland of selling out to communism, but he was also the man who had led the Finnish delegation at the peace talks in 1920, was known as an advocate of peaceful co-existence with Russia, and had a knowledge of the Russian language and of Russian conditions that was rare in a Finn. Paasikivi got his instructions on 9 October and set off for Moscow. The instructions were such that almost no scope for bargaining existed, for they started from the premise that Finland's absolute neutrality forbade her to offer any advantages to a third power, and from the juridical fact that the existing relationship of Finland and Russia had been definitively

[1] *DGFP*, pp. 148, 195, 231, 240, 246, 293, 255.

prescribed in the peace treaty of 1920 and the non-aggression pact of 1932. Therefore Finland would not consider any rectification of the frontier, would not grant any base or military facility on her territory, and would not enter into any kind of mutual assistance treaty. As the utmost concession she would consider ceding the small islands in the Gulf of Finland in exchange for territory elsewhere.

There was nothing in the international situation in October 1939 which justified Finland in adopting this hard line. Germany had made her position plain, and Britain and France were essentially giving the same advice as Germany. The British government had already decided to overlook the Russian attack on Poland and rather welcomed Russian activity in the Baltic area. A foreign office memorandum of 19 October assumed that this activity was really anti-German and would be 'very unfavourable to German interests in the long run'. Government policy was to try to wean Soviet Russia away from her collaboration with Hitler. On 25 October Halifax was authorized by the cabinet to tell the Russian ambassador that Britain wanted to improve relations with the Soviet Union. This policy was reinforced by a report of the chiefs-of-staff to the cabinet, which was adopted on 1 November. They regarded a winter campaign against Finland as unlikely, but in any case war between Finland and Russia would be no threat to the Allies. Furthermore, there was no way in which the Allies could give effective help to the Finns, the chiefs of staff being strongly against any action that might embroil the Allies with Russia. The cabinet therefore decided that British policy should not encourage Finland to resist the Russian demands. It was true that in the United States, where the Finnish government and private interests had canvassed support, much sympathy had been loudly expressed. President Roosevelt wrote a letter to the Russian president, Kalinin, expressing the hope that nothing would happen to disturb the peaceful relations of Finland and Russia, or to endanger Finland's independence. Similarly the Scandinavian neutrals had sent a joint note to the Soviet government on 12 October, timed to coincide with the opening of the talks, in which they declared their interest in the maintenance of Finland's neutral status. But the Soviet leaders evaluated these interventions correctly as being without real significance; the brutal truth was that Finland stood quite alone in face of the Russian demands, and that in these circumstances the unyielding attitude taken up by her government showed the grave lack of political realism prevailing among its members.[2]

The Russo-Finnish negotiations of 1939, the first round of which comprised three sessions held on 12 and 14 October, were a diplomatic oddity. There was no agenda or fixed protocol; the two parties sat informally round a table and exchanged views in what was usually a friendly and relaxed atmosphere. The Russians were represented by Molotov and Stalin and the two sides proceeded to set out their respective positions. Molotov began by suggesting a mutual assistance pact such as the Baltic states had just concluded, or a more limited agreement for the joint defence of the Gulf of Finland. In either case the Russians would require territorial concessions and base facilities in Finland and these were specified. They wanted a thirty-year lease of the port of Hanko at the mouth of the Gulf of Finland, with the right to keep a garrison of 5,000 men and anchorage facilities for warships nearby. In the Gulf of Finland they wanted the cession to the Soviet Union of all the Finnish islands, including Suursaari, and on the Karelian isthmus they wanted the land frontier to be moved back some seventy kilometres further from Leningrad, and the mutual destruction of fortifications on the isthmus. Then in the far north they asked for possession of the Finnish part of the Rybachiy peninsula, which covered the approaches to Finland's Arctic ocean port of Liinahamari. Finally the terms of the non-aggression pact

[2] L. Woodward, *British Foreign Policy in the Second World War*, I, p. 35. (Hereafter *Woodward*).

should be revised to include an undertaking by both parties not to enter into alliances directed against the other. In return, the Soviet Union offered territory in Russian Karelia nearly twice as large as the areas to be ceded by Finland, and they would consent to Finland fortifying the Åland islands provided she did it alone. Paasikivi reported these terms back to his government and was told to stand on his instructions: Finland would not enter into a mutual assistance pact of any kind, and no territorial concessions could be offered beyond the lesser islands in the Gulf of Finland.[3]

At the main session on 14 October the Russians explained the thinking behind their demands. The modification of the frontier on the Arctic ocean was in a class by itself and was a precaution against a possible attack on Murmansk from either Britain or Germany. Both powers were openly interested in the nickel mines of Petsamo, but Molotov believed this was only a cover for their real intentions 'the purpose of both of them is to attack Murmansk'. All the other demands were related to the defence of Leningrad by closing the Gulf of Finland and moving the frontier beyond artillery range of Leningrad and Kronstadt. Stalin said:

> We must be able to shut off access to the Gulf of Finland . . . if once a hostile fleet gets in to the Gulf of Finland, it cannot be defended any longer. You ask what power would attack us? Britain or Germany. We have good relations with Germany now, but in this world everything can change . . . Both Britain and Germany can now send large naval units into the Gulf of Finland. When the war between these two is finished the fleet of the victor will come in to the Gulf of Finland . . . We cannot do anything about geography, nor can you. In Leningrad and its surroundings the population is about three and a half million, almost as big as the whole of Finland. Since Leningrad cannot be moved the frontier must move further away. We ask for 2,700 square kilometres and

---

[3] *Jakobson*, pp. 114-6: J. K. Paasikivi, *Toimintani Moskovassa ja Suomessa 1939-41*, I, pp. 37-43. (Hereafter *Paasikivi*).

we offer 5,500 square kilometres. Would any other great power do this? No. We are the only ones who are that silly.

Paasikivi interjected that 'you talk as though Finland might threaten the Soviet Union with war'. Stalin replied: 'We are not afraid of an attack by Finland, but Britain or Germany can exercise pressure to force Finland to take part in an attack on the Soviet Union.'[4]

As it was clear that Paasikivi's instructions provided no basis for a serious discussion of the Russian proposals, he asked for a delay so that he could consult his government. Stalin agreed, but he warned of the danger of prolonging the situation, 'You have mobilized and evacuated cities. Your newspapers are talking about Russian imperialism. We too have sent troops to the frontier. This situation cannot go on for long.' But this apart, there were no threats or pressure; the talks ended on a note of good humour as Molotov said 'sign an agreement with us on the twentieth and I will give you a dinner the following day.'[5]

It seems clear that Stalin believed that at the end of the European war the victorious power, whether Britain or Germany, would turn its arms against the Soviet Union – and given the state of the world in 1939 as it must have looked to Stalin, this was a plausible assumption. If this assumption is granted, then the Russian requirements were both rational and moderate, for they had affirmed solemnly that no other considerations than those of military security were involved. Molotov declared: 'We shall not lift a finger to interfere in your own affairs, nor should we touch your independence,' and later 'it is to our advantage that Finland stays neutral'. Therefore, for anyone who is willing to accept that Stalin made these proposals to Finland in good faith, it is difficult to criticize them, except on the grounds used by the Finnish delegation that they were militarily obsolete.

[4] *Paasikivi*, pp. 45-6.
[5] *Paasikivi*, p. 47.

Stalin's several allusions to the British intervention in the Baltic in 1919 suggest that his thinking about the danger to Leningrad was outdated. With air power and the bases already secured in the Baltic states, it was probably unnecessary for the Russians to have a base to the north of the Gulf of Finland as well in order to close it to hostile naval forces. History records that Leningrad has never been attacked successfully by land over the Karelian isthmus, in part because the approaches from the south are much more open and feasible for any potential aggressor. But though the Russian proposals may have been poorly conceived for their declared purpose, they were designed to meet contingencies that were not, in 1939, by any means improbable and can be taken at their face value as real attempts to meet a real situation, and not as some kind of advance cover for other, ulterior designs. Indeed, the consciousness of their good faith and moderation made the Finnish refusal to accept the proposals look perverse and incomprehensible to the Russians, and therefore ultimately suspicious or sinister.[6]

But the Russian proposals looked very different from the Finnish point of view, as became apparent when they were discussed by the leadership in a series of consultations between 16 and 20 October designed to produce a counter-offer.

It is fair to say that all the Finns involved acted in the belief that the Russian demands were not to be taken at face value, but did indeed represent a first stage in some larger design against Finland. So deep-rooted was this conviction that the very moderation of the Russian proposals was read as sinister. Thus General Oesch argued that the proposed shifting of the frontier could add nothing substantial to the security of Leningrad in the face of modern methods of warfare; on the other hand it was just enough to disrupt the prepared line of Finnish defences and render Finland less able to resist the real Russian demands that would come later. General Öhqvist took a similar view: 'No officer with a modern training

[6] *Paasikivi*, p. 47.

could take really seriously the grounds for the demands they have put to us. More likely what they are demanding is only the preparation for further, much more far-reaching demands.' This kind of thinking was shrewd and perceptive, and would have been valid but for one factor which it overlooks – Stalin was not an officer, and did not have a modern training. These reactions from two intelligent, thoroughly professional soldiers, merely illustrate the imposibility for any leading Finn to accept that Soviet leaders meant what they said. There was unanimity in the Finnish ruling circles that the proposals were a trap: the divisions arose about the best way of evading it.[7]

The majority view of most of the politicians, military advisers, and of the Finnish public was that no substantial concessions should be made. This was based on two lines of argument: the first, voiced by defence minister Niukkanen, was that any concession would be interpreted as a sign of weakness and would invite the further demands that were coming in any case. He said it was obvious that the base at Hanko was intended to facilitate a future penetration of Finland, and it would be better to fight than give in. 'Russia cannot concentrate many troops against us. The Russian attack will be a weak pressure. The political situation can change during the fighting.' Erkko made a similar assessment of Russia's real intentions; 'The Russian demands on Finnish territory are not concerned with the security of Leningrad, but are political, that is Russia's aim is to achieve the 1914 frontier.' But he went on to express the second line of argument against making concessions, the view that because Finland's position was secure in international law, Russia would not launch a war of blatant aggression. He said to Paasikivi: 'We have right on our side and Russia is bound by the treaties she has made with us in the eyes of the whole world.' Very few Finns, even today, are willing to face the contradictions in these arguments, yet they are clear enough – if the Russians were unscrupulous and had aggressive intentions, their attack

[7] R. Seppälä, *Mainilan laukaukset*, p. 38. (Hereafter *Seppälä*).

would not be a demonstration only, nor would they be in the least deterred by treaty obligations. Yet men like Erkko and Niukkanen consistently adhered to these incompatible positions, and encouraged their countrymen to do the same. They welcomed the readiness to fight rather than give way, expressed in numerous public deputations, rallies and newspaper articles, while at the same time they gave the public to understand that there was no real danger of war. Erkko told the cabinet ' I believe that even so Russia will not attack', but perhaps the full unreality of Erkko's mental world is expressed in his parting remark to Paasikivi on setting out for Moscow – 'forget that Russia is a great power'.[8]

The minority of realists on the Finnish side was led by Paasikivi and Mannerheim, and the only major political leader who gave them somewhat hesitant support was the socialist finance minister, V. Tanner. They held that an agreement must be secured because Finland had no prospect of fighting successfully and the Russians were clearly in deadly earnest – Finland must make whatever concession was necessary to avoid a conflict. Mannerheim held that it was hopeless for Finland to fight alone. 'In planning the defence of Finland we have always reckoned that if war came, Russia would be engaged elsewhere. Now the situation is quite different.' It was not the case that Mannerheim or Paasikivi had any confidence in Russia's good faith, it was simply that, to them, to choose to fight in the existing circumstances looked suicidal. Thus Mannerheim held that if even Sweden would commit herself to fight with Finland, the situation would be quite different, and Finland could afford to stand firm, but there was no sign that Sweden would.[9]

The Finns had been hoping for some declaration of support from a meeting of Scandinavian heads of state which took place in Stockholm on 18 October, but the communiqué issued on 19 October did not mention the

[8] *Passikivi*, pp. 58, 60.
[9] *Paasikivi*, p. 60.

Finnish crisis. Instead it announced that 'the meeting unanimously stated that the governments were determined, in close cooperation, to adhere consistently to strict neutrality.' Although Erkko had spoken with the Swedish prime minister, Hansson, all he was told was that Sweden could not commit herself concerning a hypothetical situation, but that anything greater than diplomatic support was unlikely. Erkko chose to put an optimistic gloss on this when he reported back to his colleagues, and later to parliament, leaving the impression that Swedish military intervention was not ruled out. In fact the Swedish position was uncertain at this point, for there was a section of the Swedish Right and of the ruling socialists led by foreign minister Sandler, backed by the military experts, that did contemplate Swedish military intervention if Russia attacked Finland. The situation was only resolved after 26 October, when Tanner wrote to Hansson asking him bluntly whether Sweden would give assistance in case of war. The Swedish cabinet had nearly split on the question at a meeting on 22 October. Hansson had then canvassed the whole spectrum of political opinion, and on the basis of what he learned he replied to Tanner, on 27 October, that 'Sweden should not, by joining in the defence of Åland, or in any other way take the risk of being involved in a conflict with the Soviet Union.' So the Swedish attitude was clarified, and as subsequently defined it meant that Sweden would give Finland all possible backing short of going to war.[10]

When the Finnish leaders drafted their counter-proposals during meetings on 20 and 21 October, those in favour of compromise could make no impression on their colleagues. It is true that Finland recognized that in principle Russia had a case, because they did offer some small concessions: on the isthmus they would eliminate the Kuokkala bend in the frontier, which would take it twelve kilometres farther from Leningrad, against the seventy demanded by the Russians, and in the Gulf of

[10] *Tanner*, pp. 45-7: *Jakobson*, pp. 120-2: *Paasikivi*, p. 63.

Finland they would discuss sharing the island of Suur-saari. But on the question of a base at Hanko and on the Rybachiy peninsula they offered no concession at all. The suggestion of Mannerheim and Paasikivi that they should offer an off-shore island for a base instead of Hanko was rejected.[11]

When Paasikivi returned to Moscow he was accompanied, at his own request, by Tanner, for he wanted the support of a responsible political leader. The government, especially Erkko, readily agreed, because they wanted to stiffen Paasikivi, whom they regarded as soft, with a less compliant partner, as Erkko's letter to Tanner made very clear. The Finns met Stalin and Molotov again on 23 October and the Finnish proposals were rejected as totally insufficient. Stalin brushed aside the Finnish assurance that they would fight to preserve their neutrality, and said, pointing to Hanko on the map, 'a great power will land here and continue on its way regardless of your resistance'. When Tanner urged that the existing treaties formed an adequate basis for Finnish-Russian relations, Molotov replied that 'you Finns cannot expect that terms agreed in 1920 could be adequate now'. The Russians then handed over a memorandum insisting that they must have Hanko, but offering to reduce the garrison to 4,000 men, and to withdraw it at the conclusion of the European war; as regards the isthmus, they offered a modified line involving a smaller loss of territory, but still far beyond what Finland was suggesting. They insisted on all their remaining demands, except that the idea of a mutual assistance treaty was now dropped. It must be concluded that since the Russians had made concessions to the Finnish point of view, however limited, they genuinely wished for a negotiated settlement. Paasikivi certainly interpreted the proceedings this way, but his instructions did not allow for further bargaining, so the Finnish delegation had to insist on returning to Helsinki for further consultations. Stalin and Molotov were visibly discontented with this

[11] *Paasikivi*, p. 61.

delay, for Molotov let slip his first really threatening remark: 'Do you want matters to come to a conflict?' But it was agreed that there should be another break in the talks so that the Finns could get fresh instructions.[12]

The delegation was back in Helsinki on 26 October and a new round of talks began among the Finnish leaders. Mannerheim, when asked for his assessment of the possibilities in the event of war, replied that he could foresee nothing but disaster – for instance, there was only two weeks' supply of artillery ammunition. But the politicians would not listen. Niukkanen insisted that the army could hold out for six months if necessary, and after a painful argument Mannerheim left the meeting. A second professional opinion from general Österman was similarly ignored; he said 'without the slightest doubt we shall lose a war'. Niukkanen's comment to Paasikivi on this was that 'the military command is always too pessimistic'. So Erkko was allowed to draft a counter-proposal that clearly would not satisfy the Russians; a little more territory was offered on the isthmus, and something would be conceded on the Rybachiy peninsula, but that was all. The Finns would not concede Hanko or any equivalent base on the Gulf of Finland, nor give up Koivisto on the east, both of which Stalin had made clear he would insist on. To strengthen their position the government now revealed its proposals to the leaders of the parliamentary parties on 28 October. The prime-minister, Cajander, Niukkanen and Erkko all stressed that although they wanted to avoid war, it would be better to fight than give in; in Niukkanen's words 'war is more advantageous than the Russian demands'. Erkko stressed that in any case there was really no danger, 'if Finland sticks to her guns over Hanko, the Russians will climb down . . . In any case the Soviet Union will not allow a conflict to develop'. When asked about the attitude to the crisis of the Swedish government Erkko implied that it was still undecided and that intervention was not ruled out,

[12] *Paasikivi*, pp. 56, 66, 68.

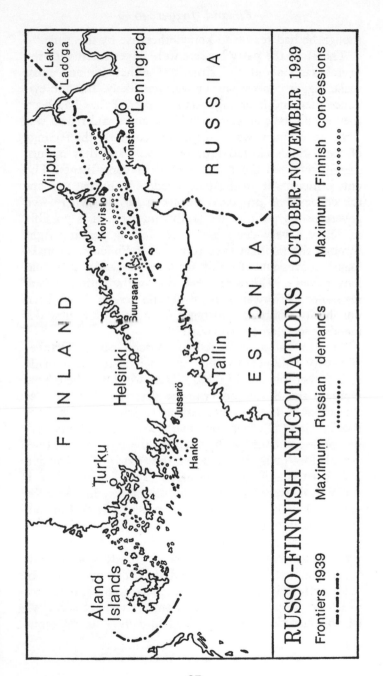

RUSSO-FINNISH NEGOTIATIONS OCTOBER–NOVEMBER 1939

Frontiers 1939   Maximum Russian demands   Maximum Finnish concessions

though he had reason to know otherwise by this time.[13]

Therefore the party leaders were never faced with the brutal truth about the situation : either Finland must make bigger concessions or war was likely. But the evidence then and later suggests that even if they had been they would have agreed with Niukkanen, and risked war – the government was interpreting correctly the feelings of the nation's elected representatives, and they in turn merely reflected the feelings of their constituents. The only criticisms from the party leaders were that perhaps the concessions proposed went too far. In general the government's position was fully endorsed. It is possible to detect a very deep instinctive feeling running right through the political spectrum that if Finland did make major concessions to the Russian demands 'it would have meant a deliberate weakening of the nation's moral resistance. Afterwards it would no longer have been possible to establish resistance if, after a time, new demands had been put forward.'[14]

The delegation returned to Moscow on 31 October with very little new to offer, and their instructions made it clear that this was Finland's 'final' word, for the official reply to the Soviet government described the offer as 'the extreme limit of concession to which we can go'. Paasikivi and Tanner, on their own responsibility, cut this phrase out before they handed the reply over. However, before their train reached the frontier the situation had been significantly changed by a speech which Molotov delivered to the Supreme Soviet, in which he published to the world the Russian demands on Finland. It is generally held that by this action he ruled out the possibility of compromise because now considerations of great power prestige would not permit Russia to draw back. Molotov had emphasized that 'the proposals are really extremely moderate and reduced to those measures which are necessary from the point of view of security', which must have been intended to convey to the Finns

[13] *Jakobson*, p. 131 : *Tanner*, p. 51 : *Paasikivi*, p. 71.
[14] E. Linkomies, *Vaikea aika*, p. 42. (Hereafter *Linkomies*).

that Stalin had not been bluffing when he described them
as a basic minimum. But in addition to this general warning, there were two specially significant passages in the
speech. First, Molotov said that Russia wanted 'a small
piece of territory at the mouth of the Gulf of Finland to
be used as a naval base.' The significance here was that
he did not mention Hanko by name, and this meant that
Russia was prepared to settle for some less objection-
able alternative: this was the hopeful point. The other
was less obvious but more serious, for Molotov said that
'the negotiations are being affected by the fact that the
influence of outside powers on Finland has been observ-
able.' This was serious, for the Russian leaders obviously
believed it. Leningrad Radio had asked on 1 November
'who is Finland relying on? There was another country
which also expected promised assistance and what did it
get?' The allusion to the fate of Poland was evidence that
the Soviet leaders believed that Britain and France were
inspiring Finnish obstinacy; indeed this is still the view
enshrined in the official Russian histories. A recent
account published in the Soviet Union asserts: 'In reality
ruling circles in England and France succeeded in provoking reactionary forces in Finland into war with the
Soviet Union.' The truth, as has been seen, was the
opposite: Britain had decided not to encourage Finland
to resist. Sadly, in a situation like this, the truth is not
important, what mattered was that Stalin and Molotov
believed that there had been Anglo-French interference.
Otherwise, they reasoned, why should the Finns, as presumably reasonable beings, contemplate carrying resistance to the point of war, unless they had some assurance
of outside help? This failure by the Russian leaders to
understand the mentality of their opponent had led them
to conclude that either the Finns would give way once
they were convinced that Russia was in earnest, or else
they really did have assurances of outside help and must
be dealt with quickly before this help could materialize. It
was a situation where both parties totally miscalculated
the intentions of the other, and thus were prevented from

finding a realistic basis for a settlement. Yet Molotov's message was clear enough. 'It is to be feared that the rejection of the Soviet Union's plan could bring with it serious damage for Finland. It must be hoped that Finnish ruling circles do not allow certain foreign influences hostile to the Soviet Union to incite them.'[15]

The Finnish government certainly failed to get the message; rather it was outraged by what it saw as crude blackmail which ignored the diplomatic decencies. They contemplated recalling their delegation in protest, and because the situation had significantly changed since their instructions were drafted, but in the end they left it to Paasikivi and Tanner to decide whether to proceed. They both felt that to turn back in face of the speech would be a provocative demonstration, and continued with their journey.

They met Molotov, without Stalin, on 3 November and handed over their government's reply. Molotov could only say that it offered no basis for an agreement and concluded with these words: 'So far the civilians have handled the matter and since there has been no agreement the matter will have to be given over to the military.' This was a clear threat to resort to force. Molotov's patience was exhausted, but Stalin's was not for he appeared at a meeting on 4 November to try to reach a compromise. First he suggested 'sell us Hanko if you do not want to lease it. Then the area will belong to the Soviet Union and be under its sovereignty.' The Finns replied that they could not discuss this, and Stalin repeated that Russia must have a base because Finland was too weak to defend its neutrality against a great power. Suddenly he suggested that they drop Hanko and use instead a nearby group of islands. This convinced Paasikivi and Tanner that Stalin was genuinely looking for a compromise, and they asked for time to consult their government. They could see that if Finland would offer an island for a base and some more territory on the

---

[15] *Paasikivi*, p. 72: *Seppälä*, pp. 53, 57, 79.

isthmus then an agreement was in sight and they cabled their government to this effect.[16]

The result was the opposite of what Stalin intended or Paasikivi hoped: Erkko and the politicians in Finland concluded that the Russians were weakening, and after they had again consulted the party leaders, they told the delegation to refuse a base in any form, and only if the Russians accepted this refusal to offer a further small concession on the isthmus. Paasikivi and Tanner could see that this was tantamount to rejecting the Russian terms and cabled to Helsinki: 'If no agreement on this basis can we break off the negotiations?' The reply came: 'You know we have gone as far in concession as our security and independence permit. If there is no agreement on the proposed terms, you may break off the negotiations.'[17]

The final meeting with Stalin took place on 9 November. When the Russian leader heard that his suggestion had been rejected he muttered 'nothing will come of this', and yet he made one more effort; he pointed to another island on the map and asked 'is this island vital to you?' But the Finns could only repeat they were not authorized to discuss any island at all. There was some further talk about the isthmus frontier, but here too the Finns had nothing of substance to offer and the discussion ground to a halt. Tanner then suggested that it seemed that agreement was impossible. Stalin concurred and the talks ended there. Molotov sent a letter that evening that clearly hinted that the Soviet proposal to establish a base on an island instead of Hanko was still open, but Paasikivi and Tanner had to reply that the whole idea was unacceptable, though they hoped an agreement might yet be reached on the basis of Finland's proposals. To this there was no reply, and on 13 November the delegation travelled back to Finland.[18]

Paasikivi and Tanner reported to the government on

[16] *Paasikivi*, p. 84.
[17] *Paasikivi*, p. 86.
[18] *Paasikivi*, p. 87.

15 November, and subsequently to the party leaders. They suggested that only an offer of base facilities could get the talks started up again. The government would not contemplate a fresh approach, on the contrary they were confident that the Russians would either accept the deadlock, or seek to break it themselves by further reducing their demands. The ministers, and Tanner was one, were deceived by the calm and friendly tone of the Moscow talks and the absence of threats. They should have paid more attention to the changing line of the Soviet press and radio. On 3 November, *Pravda* had written that 'the Finnish government has launched several far reaching measures which cannot be interpreted otherwise than that the country is preparing for war. We shall proceed on our way wherever it may lead us. We shall guarantee the security of the Soviet Union regardless of everything, smashing all obstacles of whatever kind in order to achieve our objective.' This became the consistent line of Soviet propaganda, with the repeated refrain that Finland was being incited by 'those forces which are well known to us, which are trying to provoke war between Germany and Soviet Russia and succeeded in destroying Poland.' Instead the Finns continued to believe that firmness would pay off in the end. Cajander made a major speech on 23 November and referred to the mounting barrage of Russian propaganda as a war of nerves. He announced defiantly: 'Finland will not submit to becoming some kind of satellite state. No war of nerves or attrition will persuade us to this, any more than fair promises . . . The present situation could go on for a long time. We must get used to living and working in these changed conditions . . . we must learn to plough with a gun on our shoulder.'[19]

As the days passed and nothing happened the government and the public became more complacent, Erkko was certain nothing would happen before the spring – 'they would not invade us in mid-winter.' Evacuees returned to the cities and the frontier zone and the

[19] *Seppälä*, pp. 65, 100.

government announced that the schools would open on 1 December. When the government met on 20 November Tanner strongly opposed any increase in military expenditures; indeed he led a group of ministers who wanted to demobilize some of the reservists, though the majority were not yet ready for this. Only the small circle of pessimists like Mannerheim and Paasikivi refused to believe that the Russians had accepted defeat and continued to nag the government about making a fresh approach to Russia. On 18 November Mannerheim expressed deep alarm to Paasikivi; he was 'very worried' and sure they must resume the negotiation. Paasikivi transmitted these opinions to the government and added his own advocacy of immediate action, but nobody would listen. Erkko told him there was nothing to fear – 'you can go on your holiday in peace'. On 26 November he tried Tanner, who agreed that something would have to be done at some time, but added that the government had no plans for an initiative in the near future. In the end, Mannerheim could stand it no longer. On 27 November he submitted his resignation as chairman of the Defence Council and commander-in-chief designate, on the grounds that he could no longer be responsible for a situation in which the government showed no appreciation of realities.[20]

It is only fair to the Finns to record that their illusions were shared by others: the Italian military attaché in Moscow told his government on 23 November that the collective view of the diplomatic corps in Moscow was that Russia would not resort to force. Hitler too was sure that war would be avoided because he shared Stalin's original belief that Finland was bound to agree to such moderate terms. He told Sven Hedin that he was certain there would not be a war, 'I do not believe that such a situation will arise', though if it did Germany would observe strict neutrality. The Germans, who alone knew the contents of the German-Soviet pact and least of all

[20] *Paasikivi*, pp. 102, 103: *Jakobson*, p. 150: G. Mannerheim, *Muistelmat*, II, pp. 129-33. (Hereafter *Mannerheim*).

wanted a war in the Baltic, continued to urge the Finns, through various channels, to make an agreement with Russia. For instance, Göring told the Finnish professor B. Wuolle that if Finland behaved reasonably Germany would 'guarantee' that there would be no further demands from the Soviet Union. The British too did not take the possibility of war very seriously, but in accordance with cabinet policy, while they gave no specific advice to Finland, indicated that the Finns would do well to accept the Russian proposals.[21]

The main reason why most observers were mistaken about Russian intentions in November 1939 was that the Russians themselves did not know what to do. Although they had been preparing for military action in Finland since late 1938, and the commander of the Leningrad military district had been working with Stalin personally on the plans for what he called a 'counter-blow' into Finland, this had been to meet the situation in which a great power was using Finland for an attack on the Soviet Union. For the actual situation which had developed in November, Stalin had no plans, since he had not envisaged that Finland would refuse his terms. The sense of bafflement felt by the Russian leaders came out in a conversation between Molotov and the German ambassador on 13 November. Molotov was reported as being 'very angry at the Finns . . . the stubbornness of the Finns could only be explained by the fact that their resistance was being bolstered by England.'[22]

But there was a group in the Russian leadership that had favoured strong action to solve the problem of Finland, and the circumstantial evidence suggests that it centered on Zhdanov, the leader of the Leningrad party. He naturally felt a more immediate concern with the Finnish question, on which he had publicly expressed himself some years previously. Zhdanov and a military lobby may have been the people Molotov had in mind on

[21] *Tanner*, p. 82: *Linkomies*, p. 49: *Jakobson*, p. 142: *DGFP*, p. 293.
[22] *DGFP*, p. 427: *Meretskov*, pp. 178-9.

3 November, when he referred to the military taking over matters from the civilians. Certainly someone in authority must have sanctioned the threatening article in *Pravda* that day, which has already been quoted. It looks as though after 9 November, when the talks broke down, Zhdanov and his group persuaded Stalin to let them try their solution. This was based on two beliefs about Finland's capacity to resist an attack by Russia. The first was that expressed by Stalin during the talks that Finland was too weak to resist an attack by a great power, even in the most favourable circumstances. The second was that in the special case of an attack by the Soviet Union there would be support for Russia among the Finnish workers and conscripts. This notion can be found in *Krasnaja Gazeta* in 1938, when it wrote that 'the Finnish army, which for the most part is made up of peasants and workers, has no desire to pour out its blood for the benefit of landowners and bourgeois . . . It is certain that if war broke out with the Soviet Union the democratic elements of the population are ready to turn their weapons against the fascists.' The Finnish communist exiles in Russia undoubtedly encouraged such illusions, and it is noteworthy that their leader, O. W. Kuusinen, had been involved in the planning process during the summer of 1939. On the basis of this analysis it would be possible for the forces of the Leningrad military district alone to smash Finnish resistance, overrun the country quickly with the collaboration of large elements of the population and set up a friendly régime led by the Finnish communist party.[23]

It is known that clearance for this plan had been given by 13 November, for on that day a courier arrived in Stockholm, where the secretary of the Finnish communist party was based, and instructed him to return to Russia for a new assignment. But Tuominen, the secretary, had been shaken in his loyalties by the purges, which had carried off so many of his comrades, and was finally shattered by the German-Soviet pact. He declined

[23] *Korhonen*, p. 205.

to go, and repeated his refusal to a second courier on 21 November. This time the plan was explained to him: there would be military action against Finland and Tuominen was to be the head of a pro-Russian government which would be installed. Tuominen's refusal to act the part allotted to him was only a minor inconvenience and it meant that O. W. Kuusinen would have to take the lead instead.[24]

Tuominen's account meshes exactly with the timing of the Russian propaganda campaign: the TASS reporter in Helsinki began to write of the disaffection of the working class and the conscripts, and claimed to have clear evidence that the Finnish government was a tool in the hands of the British imperialists, and would be used by them to attack the Soviet Union. This was the story put over to the Russian public, that Finland was being developed by the imperialists as a base for their predatory designs against the Soviet Union. It has always been the Rusian justification for the war and the fact that there is no concrete evidence to support it has never deterred them from advancing it. Its usefulness lies in the way in which it explains why Finland was insane enough to attack the Soviet Union, and why the Russian forces met serious set-backs in the subsequent campaign, because of the scale of Anglo-French military preparations and assistance. Since Soviet historians cannot afford the luxury of telling the truth about the Russo-Finnish war, this particular fabrication represents as good a substitute as could be devised.

By 26 November the preparations were far enough advanced for the starting signal to be given. In *Pravda* there appeared a vicious attack on Cajander, who was described as a puppet of the imperialists, a clown and a cunning beast of prey. The Finnish people were urged to rid themselves of him and his government if they wanted to avoid disaster. That same evening the Finnish

[24] *Seppälä*, p. 95: *Jakobson*, pp. 144-8: A. Tuominen, *Kremlin kellot*, pp. 389-90: A. Tuominen, *Myrskyn aika*, pp. 57-9. (Hereafter *Tuominen*).

ambassador was summoned by Molotov and handed a protest note. This claimed that Finnish artillery had fired over the frontier into the village of Mainila, killing four Russian soldiers and wounding nine. The incident showed that the presence of Finnish forces close to the frontier was not only a threat to Leningrad 'but is itself a hostile act'. The note went on 'it is not the intention of the Soviet government to exaggerate this deplorable aggression, carried out by Finnish army units which perhaps were badly directed, but it would wish that such deplorable actions should not happen in future'. Therefore it demanded that Finnish forces be withdrawn twenty-five kilometres from the frontier.[25]

There is one certainty about the alleged incident and that is that seven shots were indeed fired into Mainila at the time stated. The Finnish frontier guards, who had a clear view of the place where they landed, had made a note of them. Finland claimed, however, that the shots came from the Russian side of the border and that in any case there was no Finnish artillery near enough to the frontier to have carried that far. It is therefore likely that the truth about the Mainila shots will never be known. It could just have been a genuine accident arising from a Russian artillery practice, but all the circumstantial evidence points to a deliberate, staged provocation. That very night massive public demonstrations against the Finnish war-mongers were said to have taken place all over the Soviet Union, and these would scarcely have happened spontaneously in Stalin's Russia. A typical account of reactions among the soldiers on the isthmus claims that after the news of the shooting got around 'nobody ordered the men to meet . . . A meeting began. The well-known tank-man, Fedor Dudko, appeared as the first speaker: "Our patience is at an end. We expect battle-orders from our government to put a bridle in the mouth of these run-away war-mongers . . ." Non-commissioned Officer Lupov went towards the rostrum but while he was climbing up he yelled impatiently "What is the use of a lot of talk? Let's send our tanks into battle first".' If these and many similar accounts describe anything that really happened, they would suggest that the official propaganda had done its work among the men of the Red Army.[26]

Yet there remains some slight ambiguity about the intentions of the Russian government even at this point, for the note, in speaking of a desire not to exaggerate the incident, may be held to have included a let-out clause. At least that was how Paasikivi saw it, for he noted in his diary that 'it does not contain any threats. It is fairly moderate in its demands.' It may be that the Cajander government was being offered one last chance to submit and meet Russian requirements, but it is equally possible that the seeming moderation was intended solely to impress outside observers. The point was not put to the test because the Finnish government did not submit: if they met the Russian demand it would imply that they also accepted the truth of the Russian version of the Mainila shots, and the Finnish government had evidence that this version was false. This was set out in the Finnish reply of 27 November, and then they added an innocent but misjudged suggestion that although Finland was completely innocent of any offence, she was ready to discuss a mutual withdrawal of troops from the frontier area. This gave Molotov a handle for his next note on 28 November, which claimed that the Finnish reply had simply demonstrated 'the Finnish government's deep hostility to the Soviet Union and leads to the most extreme tension in the relations between the two countries.' Then he went on to make his debating point. The proposal for a mutual withdrawal of forces was absurd; the Russians would find themselves in the suburbs of Leningrad. The proposal simply showed the continuing ill-will of the Finnish government and the Soviet government therefore renounced the non-aggression pact between the two countries.[27]

[26] *Seppälä*, pp. 107, 109, 114, 119, 124.
[27] *Paasikivi*, pp. 104, 105.

The matter was now settled. Meretskov says that he had got orders to activate the plans for the 'counter-blow' as soon as he reported the Mainila shots to Moscow, but in fact they seem to have been issued on 28 November and were 'to be ready against any surprises and immediately to throw back any possible fresh attacks on the part of the Finnish troops.' At this point, when it was too late, the Finnish government for the first and last time in the crisis came down to earth and accepted that the Russians were in deadly earnest. On 29 November they despatched a further note agreeing to a unilateral withdrawal of forces, and instructed the ambassador to add that they were also ready to re-open discussions on other questions and had fresh proposals to make. By the time this reached Moscow, the ambassador had been summoned to the Kremlin and handed a statement breaking off diplomatic relations. An order of the day had been issued to the Leningrad military district 'to liquidate the most dangerous seat of war and secure the north-west frontier of the Soviet Union and the security of Leningrad for all time.' Finally Molotov, at the same time as the ambassador tried to contact him in order to present his new note, had gone on the air with an address to the Russian people.[28]

He said that the basic hostility of the existing Finnish government, which was relying on its relations with the imperialist powers, had been fully demonstrated. 'The present Finnish government, which has become involved with imperialist powers hostile to the Soviet Union, does not want to preserve normal relations with the Soviet Union.' Russia had been obliged to take steps to secure itself. 'The only aim of our measures is to guarantee the safety of the Soviet Union and especially of Leningrad . . . In the present international situation, made acute by the war, we cannot leave the resolution of this task, of vital and urgent importance to the state, dependent on the ill-will of Finland's rulers.' But Russia had no quarrel with the 'real Finland', on the contrary

[28] *Meretskov*, pp. 182-3: *Seppälä*, p. 140.

she was ready to discuss transferring Soviet Karelia to the Finnish people. But for this to happen 'it was essential that the Finnish government, in its relations to the Soviet Union adopted not a hostile, but a friendly attitude, so that there could be unanimity over the great problems of concern to both peoples . . . We consider Finland, whatever sort of government she may have, as an independent and sovereign state in all matters . . . The peoples of our country are still ready to help the Finnish people to secure its free and independent development . . .' Thus the stage was set for the appearance of a friendly Finnish 'government', which the Soviet government would assist in realizing the true aspirations of the Finnish people.[29]

On the morning of 30 November, Russian ground forces began to cross the frontier at several points and Soviet bombers raided Helsinki. The war had begun. Mannerheim withdrew his resignation and was appointed commander-in-chief of the Finnish forces. But Paasikivi's diary for that day made a bitter comment on what had happened: 'This is what we have come to. We have allowed our country to slide into war with the giant Soviet Union although the following facts are before us: (1) Nobody has promised us any help. (2) The Soviet Union has its hands free. (3) Our defence forces are seriously defective. Really this is scarcely a purposeful foreign policy – Our ship of state has lacked leadership. We have slid unreflectingly into war and misfortune.' It had now to be shown whether the Finnish people and their army could to any extent redeem the disaster their leaders had brought upon them.

[29] *Seppälä*, p. 152: *Paasikivi*, p. 116.

III

The Russo-Finnish War, Phase One
The Russian Failure

Ultimately, Finland's defensive capacity was governed by the size of her population, which in 1939 was a little under four million. This gave the theoretical possibility of raising an army of fifteen infantry divisions of 14,200 men each, together with the necessary specialist and auxiliary units. Successive governments, however, had never been willing to provide the money needed to equip an army of this size, and in consequence there were only nine divisions ready for service, a tenth division for which there were only small arms and no heavy equipment, and the possibility of raising two further divisions if the equipment could be found. Thus, for actual fighting purposes, the Finnish army had nine divisions, the country being divided into nine military districts, each of which supplied one division. These districts had a permanent staff and depots and on the issue of mobilization telegrams the reservists reported to the depots, picked up their equipment and were ready to move to the front. In time of peace there was only a skeleton standing army, under cover of which the field army was to be mobilized; the backbone consisted of a small cadre of professional officers and NCOs, who were the only full-time professional soldiers. To these were added the yearly intake of conscripts, produced by the twelve-month military service. This peace-time army, organised in brigades, was the covering force and in war its function was to hold up the enemy for the two weeks required to mobilize the field army and move it into position. It was a sensible defensive scheme and on the whole it worked well, but there were built-in weaknesses. It was very rare for a field army division to be mobilized for training in time of peace, mainly because of the expense involved; this meant that the officers who would command the division in war were not familiar with all their troops and had little practice in handling the larger units under active service conditions. Officers who had been accustomed to commanding companies suddenly found themselves in charge of battalions under war conditions and had to adjust as they went along. But this sort of thing was probably inevitable for a small country in Finland's position, and there was no better way known for such a country to meet its defence problems.

Without doubt the prospects of a successful defence could have been greatly improved by a more generous provision of equipment and training facilities. Both had been skimped in order to save money, and the former further held back by arguments over what kind of equipment the forces should have, and where it was to be produced. The infantry were short of automatic weapons. They were equipped with the Suomi machine-pistol, a sub-machine gun devised in Finland for local conditions and very effective within these limits. There were, however, only 250 of these to a division, supplementing the 116 orthodox machine-guns which a Finnish division possessed (comparable to the 200 machine-guns of a Russian rifle division). Moving up the scale of equipment, the Finnish division had eighteen 81-mm mortars, and should also have had some 120-mm mortars, but these had not yet been provided. They were victims of the policy, favoured by the government against military advice, of waiting to produce the weapons in Finland rather than importing them. The Finnish artillery was similarly deficient in both quantity and quality. There were thirty-six guns assigned to each division, but they were all pre-1918 models with comparatively short range and a slow rate of fire. This meant that they were of little use for counter-battery work as they had insufficient range to reach the opposing artillery. There was a reserve of 174 even older guns, but these were really museum pieces. Delays in selecting an appropriate weapon, and insistence that it be produced at home, had left the army almost denuded of anti-tank guns. The Swedish Bofors

37-mm gun had been chosen, but only 100 of these had been issued to the troops when war began, though production was beginning to reach a satisfactory level. These guns were supplemented by guns from the Swedish government stocks, but there was a shortage of adequately trained crews.

For all practical purposes the Finnish army had no armour. Apart from some tanks of 1918 vintage, which were unusable, they had thirty Vickers light tanks, which had only just been armed and were not really serviceable at the outbreak of war. The absence of tanks did not matter very much; Finnish conditions generally were not favourable to tank warfare, but what did matter was that the Finnish infantry had literally no experience of tanks and no training in working with them or against them. In view of the shortage of anti-tank weapons this might have caused a disaster. The Finnish army had no anti-aircraft guns at all: these had met the same problems as the anti-tank gun and there were only 100 of them at the outbreak of war, all committed to the defence of the cities. In addition, economy campaigns had left the army short of such necessities as uniforms, tents and medical supplies, and virtually without any communications equipment more sophisticated than field telephones. The lack of wireless, and a consequent dependence on runners when the telephone lines were disrupted, or when units were on the move, was a grave weakness of the Finnish army.

The air force was tiny; there were about 100 machines but some of these were unfit for service. The forty-eight fighters were not of the most modern type and neither were the thirty-four reconnaissance aircraft and there were only eighteen modern twin-engined bombers. Finland did not produce any aircraft and there were no reserve machines, while the money available in peacetime had allowed only ten hours flying a month for each pilot. In effect the army had to operate without air cover or support. The navy too was insignificant, but fortunately the sea was frozen for most of the war and no serious naval operations were possible. There was an effective system of coastal defence batteries inherited from Tsarist times which adequately covered most of the vunerable points. Finally there were deficiencies in stocks and reserves: the artillery began the war with 200,000 rounds of light artillery ammunition and 70,000 heavy rounds – an average of 640 shells per gun. The Russians were capable of firing off this quantity of artillery ammunition in a single day of full-scale fighting, and even at the end of the war domestic shell production was only 3,500 rounds a day. So the Finnish artillery, in addition to being short of guns, did not have enough shells to make full use of those that it did have.[1]

There were two factors which compensated to some extent for these numerous deficiencies in material. The first was the existence of a prepared line of defence on the Karelian isthmus, the main and most vulnerable theatre of war. This defensive belt is invariably referred to as the Mannerheim Line, but the implied comparison with the Maginot Line is quite misleading. The defensive front across the isthmus was about seventy kilometres long with its two flanks anchored on the very effective heavy batteries of Koivisto in the west and Kaarnajoki and Ylläpää at the lake Ladoga end – the only fortress artillery the line possessed. The river Vuoksi, a formidable natural barrier, covered the eastern third of the position. Between the Vuoksi and the Gulf of Finland there were broad stretches of lake and swamp, which were natural obstacles in summer, but rather the contrary when frozen in winter, and, between the swamps and lakes, stretches of open country through which the roads and railway passed. Consequently, while the whole front was covered with a fairly continuous system of fieldworks, trenches, wire and tank obstacles, and sometimes by minefields, only the most vulnerable sectors, totalling about a third of the whole, had concrete fortifications. These were of two kinds: seventy-five concrete bunkers

[1] *Mannerheim*, pp. 148-151: W. Halsti, *Suomen sota*, I, pp. 40-68. (Hereafter *Halsti*).

and pill-boxes built in the 1920s and obsolete by 1939, since they could not withstand modern shellfire; and forty-four modern concrete bunkers. Russian accounts, which have their own reasons for exaggerating, claim that these structures were virtually shellproof, being immune to direct hits from 203-mm shells, and were of great depth and sophistication. Finnish descriptions make them sound much more modest, but there is no doubt they were sturdy constructions, and offered protection against enemy bombardment and against the severity of the climate. But there were never more than three such positions to a kilometre of front, and this meant there was little possibility of crossfire and mutual support. Further, the machine-guns in the bunkers were old fashioned with a slow rate of fire, and they had no anti-tank guns. Thus the Mannerheim Line was basically an ordinary trench system with tank barriers, and had nothing comparable with the concrete gun positions which were the backbone of the Maginot Line.

The second factor, through which the Finns could compensate for lack of material, was the quality of manpower – the superior skill and morale of the individual soldier. The Finnish army had had the courage to break away from orthodox continental military traditions and had evolved its own tactics based on local conditions. Most of the frontier area was a wilderness of lake and forest crossed by infrequent, poor-quality roads. If the roads could be blocked, then troops who knew how to move across the wilderness could strike at the flanks and rear of a road-bound mechanized army, which could not move into the forest nor find room for orthodox deployment. The Finnish army was trained to move fast across any kind of terrain, to avoid head-on clashes, to strike always at the flank and rear of an enemy and to make flexibility and movement compensate for numerical inferiority. In winter conditions this meant, above all, that the Finnish soldiers moved on skis, and all Finns are accustomed to skiing in forest conditions from childhood. Further, the Finns are individualists, both by temperament and tradition, so these tactics achieved the perfect match between the natural fighting qualities of the Finnish soldier and his native environment. The astonishing performance of the Finnish army in the field owes much to this striking example of the application of intelligence to the solution of problems. In addition to this, the Finnish soldier had the advantage that he knew what he was supposed to be fighting for and identified readily with his cause. He saw himself as defending his home territory and his distinctive way of life against an alien invader whom he had been taught to think of as the perpetual and implacable enemy of his nation. His most deep-rooted and basic instincts told him that this was a simple life-or-death struggle for everything he valued, and he fought accordingly.

The Russian forces were quite different. The usual figure quoted for the size of the Red Army in 1939 is 180 divisions, but this means nothing; large forces were permanently committed and only a fraction of this number were available for use against Finland. In the event about forty-five Russian divisions were used against the Finns during the war, but the number engaged at any one time was much less than this. On the other hand, a Russian rifle division, with 18,000 men, was bigger than a Finnish division and far more lavishly equipped: it had three times as much artillery, and forty or fifty tanks attached to it, where the Finns had none. In addition the Russians had abundant radio equipment, motor transport and unlimited supplies of ammunition. Further they had specialized armoured and artillery units to reinforce their rifle-divisions, together with virtually unchallenged control of the air. Altogether the Russians used 1,200,000 men, 1,500 tanks and 3,000 aircraft in the Finnish campaign; overwhelmingly superior in both manpower and material. The Russian commentators concede that the ratio of strength in their favour was two and a half to one in infantry and three to one in artillery, and in armour this ratio was overwhelming, and these are certainly underestimates. Against this it must be remembered that the Russians were generally on the offensive and that it is an accepted ground-rule of modern warfare that a successful and sustained offensive requires a superiority of at least three to one.[2]

While it is fairly easy to compare the crude material resources of the two sides, the question of quality is much more difficult to assess. The general verdict of both sides, borne out by the actual course of the fighting, is that the Russian troops proved unable to use their material superiority to good effect. Both sides also point to defective training as a key factor; the troops had not been trained for the job they had to do. The Russian soldiers were not at home in either the forest environment or the extremely severe winter climate. On the whole the Russians avoided the forest and clung to the roads and clearings, which meant they were funnelled down a series of ravines, leaving their flanks open to harassment by the Finns moving through the forest. The climate should have been no surprise to the Russians, yet the records show that they lacked white camouflage clothing, that they had very few competent ski troops, so that in any case they were bound to the roads once the deep snows began, and that their weapons and equipment were inadequately protected against low temperatures – this particular failure seems inexplicable except as gross negligence and incompetence.

Not only were the Russians poorly trained for these specific conditions, but they also showed signs that the general level of training was inadequate, the most obvious of these signs being the poor coordination of the different arms of the service. In the first phase of the war, the infantry, tanks, artillery and aircraft did not support one another's efforts with success, and this in spite of the Russian service manuals which prescribed in detail how such cooperation was to be achieved. Meretskov, the Russian commander on the isthmus, cites the example of the tank general D. G. Pavlov, who would not permit artillery to give close support to the infantry, be-

[2] *Meretskov*, p. 180.

cause he wanted to race ahead with his tanks. A further sign of poor training was the clumsy and rigid tactics, seen at their worst in the infantry. They seemed reluctant to deploy and tended to move in dense masses which simply invited slaughter by machine-guns and artillery. This kind of clumsiness is a hallmark of poorly trained troops, and compares with the similar incompetence of the Kitchener armies on the Western Front in 1915 and 1916. The artillery displayed the same kind of fault. They tended to fire to a rigid fixed pattern, and plainly preferred shooting over open sights, which they could often do with impunity because of the weakness of the opposing artillery. The reasons why the Russian troops used in Finland were poorly trained must necessarily be speculative. One explanation may be found in the prevailing military system; the Russian army had been unable to cope with the numbers of conscripts coming forward each year and only a proportion of the men had been embodied in cadre units and brought to a high level of preparedness. The rest were put in territorial units of much lower quality. There is considerable evidence that when forces were mobilized for the Finnish campaign both kinds of troops were mixed in the same units, with deplorable effects on morale and effectiveness. The greatest unknown factor is the effect of the great purge which had destroyed so many of the experienced and fully professional officers. It is certain that many Russian officers in 1939 were raw recruits and that, in view of the purge, they were understandably fearful of taking any steps without the approval of the political commissars attached to each unit. This may have had much to do with the inability of the Russians to modify their plans to meet changed circumstances: there is evidence to suggest that the natural initiative of the leaders was stifled, and they sought security in a rigid adherence to pre-set plans.

The Russian air force was a particular disappointment, and its efforts feeble by comparison with what the German air force had just achieved in the Polish campaign in similar conditions of almost uncontested control of the air. In the Finnish case air activity had only a marginal effect on the outcome of the fighting. It is true that the Finns were helped by weather conditions that often made flying impossible and that the long hours of winter darkness further restricted activity. The Finnish army had generally to try to keep out of sight during daylight and to move about on the roads only at night, but this was never more than a nuisance for it. The Russians were unable to develop effective bombing of front-line positions, and their widespread air activity behind the front brought disappointing results. Quite a lot of damage was done in the larger towns, like Helsinki and Turku, but the Russians failed either to damage industrial production to any serious extent or to impede communications, in particular the railways on which the Finns were largely dependent. And whatever allowance is made for the skill of Finnish anti-aircraft gunners and pilots, the Russian loss of about 800 aircraft looks high and suggests poor quality in both machines and their crews. The one important contribution of the Russian air force was the air drops it carried out for troops cut off along the eastern front, for without them some of these forces would have been starved out. An official German assessment of Russian military capacity, made in Decemeber 1939, was probably near the mark. It described the Russian armed forces as 'in quantity a gigantic military instrument' but went on to describe 'organization, equipment and means of leadership unsatisfactory . . . leadership itself . . . too young and inexperienced . . . the Russian mass is no match for an army with modern equipment and superior leadership.'[3]

Such were the protagonists in the Russo-Finnish war, yet for all the defects of the Red Army it looked a hopelessly uneven struggle. A superficial reading of the map would suggest that the Finns had no chance to defend a frontier of 1,000 kilometres against an enemy three

[3] J. Erikson, *The Soviet High Command*, p. 548. (Hereafter *Erikson*).

times as strong and much better equipped. But in this case the map is deceptive. The long eastern frontier, stretching north from Lake Ladoga to the Arctic Ocean was a wilderness of swamp, lake, forest and tundra, quite impenetrable by a modern army. The few poor quality roads were so hemmed in by forest and lake that an advancing column could not deploy; thus comparatively small detached units could block most of these roads against vastly greater numbers. The main Finnish army could therefore concentrate on the defence of the Karelian isthmus and the area immediately north of Lake Ladoga which secured the isthmus positions from penetration from the rear. The Finns could commit most of their nine divisions to these crucial sectors, leaving small covering forces to deal with the rest. The geographical conditions also meant that the Russians could attack with only a limited number of troops at one time because there was not space in which to deploy them, nor roads and railways to supply unlimited forces. The Finnish military planners had calculated that the Rusians could use only twelve divisions at once, seven on the isthmus and five more on the eastern front. It was a perfectly feasible proposition for an army of nine divisions, operating defensively in conditions which favoured it, to hold off such an enemy for a substantial period of time. In the long run, of course, attrition – the fact that the Russians had unlimited replacements and the Finns did not – would be decisive. But the Finns had never contemplated fighting alone for long; they had expected that other powers would come to their help if they could hold out for a reasonable time against the initial assault.

The actual situation in November 1939 was worse than the Finns had anticipated in two respects. Firstly, the European war had created a situation where no foreign assistance was in prospect, and therefore eventual defeat was almost certain, though on the other hand the very uncertainties of a general war meant that the circumstances might change very quickly, as indeed they did in the end. Secondly, the work which the Russians had done on their communications and base facilities since the end of 1938 meant that they could maintain larger forces in the field than the Finns had reckoned on. At the peak of the Russian effort against Finland they had twenty-six divisions in action, though they could not all be deployed in the front line at once, and the most serious consequence was that north of Ladoga the Russians were fielding twelve divisions instead of the expected five. Even so, given the advantages of the terrain for the defenders, and the tactical superiority of the Finns, there were still reasonable prospects of holding the attack for some time. But, balancing these adverse factors, one circumstance favoured the Finns. They had expected to have to fight a desperate holding action near the frontier with their peace-time army for the two weeks which the field army needed to mobilize and move into position. But because they had been able to mobilize undisturbed during October, the whole Finnish army was ready and in position when hostilities broke out. Indeed they had had most of four weeks for training and improvement of their defences and this was a valuable and unexpected bonus, for it enabled the covering force of the peace-time army to be formed into a tenth division, since it had not been expended in the opening stages of the war.

The Finnish order of battle on 30 November was the following: the Karelian isthmus was defended by the Karelian Army under Lieutenant-General Österman, which consisted of two army corps. On the right was the II Army Corps of Lieutenant-General Öhqvist, occupying the sector from the Gulf of Finland to the Vuoksi river, with three field army divisions on the Mannerheim line, and three groups of covering troops in front of it, consisting of the cavalry brigade, three Jäger battalions of elite light infantry and some units of the Defence Corps, a home-guard type force and the regular frontier guards. On the left was the III Army Corps of Major-General Heinrichs, with two field army divisions on the line of the Vuoksi and a covering force of one Jäger battalion, Defence Corps and frontier guards out in advance. In addition, Österman had as his army reserve the division of Major-General Laatikainen, formed from the peace-time troops and therefore an elite force.

North of Lake Ladoga Major-General Hägglund commanded the IV Army Corps with two field army divisions and the local Defence Corps and frontier guards, and covered the sector from Ladoga to Ilomantsi. To the north of this, Major-General Tuompo commanded a collection of battalions and companies which formed the North Finland Group, and covered every road over the frontier up to the Arctic Ocean. Mannerheim as commander-in-chief had his headquarters at Mikkeli, and held two field army divisions as his strategic reserve, one near Viipuri, the other at Oulu, but this was the division for which there was no artillery or heavy equipment, and it was not therefore fully operational.

The Finnish war plan called for fighting a delaying action in front of the Mannerheim line. Mannerheim himself wanted this to be a serious encounter and had urged Österman on 3 November to put strong forces in the forward area between the line and the frontier. Mannerheim had hoped to be able to win some early, morale-boosting successes in this way, but it seems his advice had not been followed, and in the event there was to be only a brief fighting retreat by the covering troops. Only on the sector between Lake Muolaanjärvi and the Vuoksi had the field army forces been pushed forward in front of the main position. The Finnish command had considered a general advance of the field army to a more forward position but had abandoned the idea—there was a shortage of tents and the troops needed the bunkers and dugouts of the main position as billets. North of Ladoga, IV Army Corps was to let the Russians advance along the lake shore, then block them and counter-attack against their flank and rear. The North Finland Group would follow a similar strategy, establishing effective road blocks and then harassing the invading columns. If reserves could be found it was hoped that these columns might be completely cut off and destroyed.[4]

The main Russian force, on the Karelian isthmus, was VII Army under General Meretskov. At full strength this consisted of twelve rifle divisions, a mechanized army corps and three tank brigades, but it was not fully mobilized when operations began as three of its divisions were still forming. To the north of Ladoga was VIII Army facing Hägglund's troops, with six rifle divisions and two tank brigades; northward again were the five rifle divisions of IX Army. These were operating in three separate columns completely detached from one another and depending precariously on the scanty roads leading west from the Murmansk railway. It was a bold operation to launch so large a force on such a deficient supply line, and one that led straight to disaster. Finally, XIV Army based on Murmansk had three rifle divisions. The Russian plan was for a rapid general advance on all fronts ending in the occupation of the whole of Finland, indeed, Meretskov says that they anticipated that a few weeks would be quite sufficient time for this. On the isthmus the Russians would assault the Mannerheim line, capture Viipuri and turn west towards Helsinki, while the VIII Army would come round Lake Ladoga and take the Finnish defences in the rear. The three columns of IX Army would seek to cut Finland in two and seal off the Swedish frontier, while XIV Army mopped up the Petsamo area and secured it against any attempt at outside intervention coming through the Arctic Ocean. It would have been a devastating plan had it been prepared and executed by troops who were equal to the demands which it made. As it was, the scope and power of the attacks in the north took the Finns by surprise and upset their dispositions. Meretskov's own account, however, shows how the preparations were rushed; he was allowed only four days after Mainila to begin operations when his original timetable called for a week of preparation, and the whole enterprise was based on a fundamental underestimation of the capacity

[4] *Halsti*, pp. 74-8: *Mannerheim*, pp. 153-5.

of the enemy. Everything points to a serious Russian belief that the Finnish conscripts would not put up a serious fight, and that significant elements among them would welcome the Red Army as liberators. Meretskov says that military intelligence had been largely neglected, and that he was given no reliable information about the Finnish army or its defences. The whole conduct of the first Russian attack is in marked contrast with what the Russians achieved in February after they had begun to take their opponent seriously and prepared their operations adequately.[5]

Hostilities began early on 30 November with artillery fire all along the frontier and air raids on the interior, and soon Russian troops were advancing. The Finnish military authorities were fully prepared and on the alert, but the civil authorities were not. They had been allowing evacuees to return to the war zone and so there were columns of civilians, often driving livestock with them blocking the roads. Fortunately the Russians came on slowly, making ten kilometres at most on the first day, although the Finnish covering forces were outnumbered by ten to one, and the Finns were able to fight a delaying action until 5 December, by the evening of which day the Russians were in contact with the Mannerheim line positions. Meretskov explains his slow advance largely in terms of mines. He claims that the evacuated areas were 'literally sown with mines' and admits that 'the soldiers were afraid to advance'. The Finnish accounts give a different impression: their big worry was tanks, which caused occasional panics among troops unfamiliar with them. There was one such panic on the night of 5 December, perhaps set off by the appearance of the Finnish army's only armoured car. A cry of 'tanks are coming' caused a retreating column to flee in panic, abandoning all its equipment, until the men got behind the main position. Fortunately there were no tanks and the abandoned equipment could be recovered, but it showed a state of nerves that was worrying. Yet it

[5] *Meretskov*, pp. 181, 182: *Erikson*, pp. 543-4.

was during these early days that the Finnish soldiers learned to cope with tanks. They found the new 37-mm anti-tank guns effective, though not as manoeuvrable as they would have wished, but above all they learned how infantry could tackle tanks at close quarters with mines and petrol bombs, which became a favourite weapon. These could only be used effectively under cover of darkness, or against tanks that were separated from their infantry, but this was precisely how the Russians were operating. Mannerheim ordered each unit down to company level to form a special anti-tank section, and with experience these became highly effective; after the first encounters the Finns coped with tanks without too much difficulty. In general the Finns found their enemy slow and unenterprising. The Russians plodded ahead along their main axis of advance, with little attempt at manoeuvring, and it was the sheer weight of numbers spilling over and round the Finnish positions that forced the defenders to pull back. Mannerheim and some of his higher commanders thought that this clumsiness could have been punished by a more aggressive defence, but the local Finnish commanders were too acutely aware of the meagreness of their reserves, and too doubtful of the offensive capacity of their troops to take the risk.[6]

On the whole the preliminary operations on the isthmus had gone much as the Finns had expected, or rather better, but on the eastern front things did not develop quite as anticipated. Two Russian divisions advanced along the shore of Lake Ladoga and were brought to a halt before the prepared position Kitelä-Syskyjärvi by 10 December. The Finnish plan then called for a counter-attack on their lines of communication, coming from the north, but this was endangered by the developments around Suojärvi, where a Russian advance threatened to turn the flank of IV Army Corps. Two Russian divisions, a much larger force than had been expected, easily pushed back the covering forces

[6] *Meretskov*, p. 183: *Halsti*, p. 100: *Mannerheim*, pp. 156-7.

round Suojärvi, and on 3 December Mannerheim ordered that they be thrown back. A Finnish regiment was rushed up and collided with the tanks of the advancing Russians. The result was catastrophe, an eye-witness describing the Finnish troops fleeing in panic as 'not hearing the shouts and curses of the officers'. Fortunately there was a prepared defensive position to their rear at Kollaa, and the Russians failed to pursue, so that it was 7 December before they tried to break through this position. The interval was just long enough for the Finns to get some artillery up, and rally their men, and after three days fighting the Russians gave up and the Kollaa position was held. But one of the Russian divisions had turned aside towards Tolvajärvi, brushing aside Finnish resistance, and Mannerheim had to intervene. He took a regiment from one of his reserve divisions, and a battalion of replacement troops, and on 6 December gave command of the Tolvajärvi sector to Colonel P. Talvela. He organized a brilliant attack against the rear of the Russian column on the night of 8/9 December, and inflicted enough damage to stop its further advance.[7]

To the north of this the Russian 54 Division was advancing on Kuhmo and again the Finnish covering force was too weak: on 3 December Mannerheim had to take a regiment from the reserve division at Oulu, which had no artillery, and send it to the Kuhmo sector. This regiment was rushed straight from the train into a counter-attack on 8 December and for a time it had the Russian column cut off, but weariness and twenty degrees of frost blunted the impetus of the Finns and the Russians were able to re-open their supply route. However, their advance had been stopped and the front stabilized. Thus two threatening situations had been saved, after the Russians had achieved strategic surprise through the strength of their advance, but in the process Mannerheim had committed nearly a third of his strategic reserve, an ominous sign after only ten days of the campaign. This was not the end of the process, however.

[7] *Halsti*, p. 114.

The Russian 163 Division had crossed the frontier and advanced on Suomussalmi, at the narrowest part of Finland, with the clear intention of cutting the country in two. The covering force could not hold them, and on 7 December the village of Suomussalmi had been evacuated. That day Mannerheim ordered the commander of 9 Division, at Oulu, to take what remained of its strength and proceed to Suomussalmi. By 9 December the troops began to arrive and the situation was temporarily stabilized, but still more of the Finnish strategic reserve had been committed to battle.

In the far north the pattern repeated itself. The Finns had supposed that the Russians could not maintain any considerable force to attack in the direction of Salla, but in fact the 122 Division came up and moved forward with dangerous ease. The danger here was that Kemijärvi might fall and the forces in the Petsamo area be cut off. To meet this the Lapland Group was formed under Major-General Wallenius on 12 December from all the available local units, and this force, helped by the onset of the Arctic winter which disrupted Russian supplies, had halted the advance by 20 December, and by vigorous harassing activity compelled the Russians to dig in. On the Arctic Ocean, a Russian division advanced on Petsamo and easily pushed the Finnish defenders back down the Arctic highway leading into the interior, thus cutting Finland off from this access to the outside world. But the further the Russians advanced, and the more severe the winter became, the slower they moved—by 16 December the Finns had stabilized a front at Höyhenjärvi, which they succeeded in holding to the end of the war. Thus by about 20 December the long eastern front had been secured, but at the cost of about half of Mannerheim's strategic reserve, and it was tying down far more of the Finnish troops than had been reckoned on. It will be seen how the Finns tried to get free of this burden.

After the Russian forces on the isthmus had come up to the Mannerheim line on 6 December they had to pause before trying to force it, and in fact it was ten days before all their units were in position and the problems of the attack had been studied. In this period there was vigorous patrol activity, with the Russians trying to establish breaches in the wire and the tank obstacles. The Russian attack concentrated on two sections of the line; at the eastern end they tried to drive across the Vuoksi at Taipale – presumably a holding attack to pull in the Finnish reserves. Then, in the centre they tried to break through on the Summa sector, where the natural obstacles were weakest, and where they could hope to develop a rapid advance on Viipuri. These thrusts were not synchronized: at Taipale the Russians started as soon as they were ready. The operations showed the Russians at their worst, for there was no element of surprise and the Finns were waiting for them. The Finnish guns were silent during the Russian artillery preparation, but opened up on the attacking infantry as soon as they began to move, with the result that the initial Russian assault on Taipale on 16 December did not gain any foothold in the Finnish position. The following day a fresh division was sent in to repeat the performance with equal lack of success, after which the Russians gave up. While the offensive raged on the Summa sector, the Russians on the Vuoksi stayed quiet, but on 25 December they renewed their effort a little to the north of the original sector. This time they did succeed in getting men across the frozen river, and even surprised and overran a Finnish battery on the further bank, but in the end this attack too was abandoned on 27 December with the Finnish positions intact. Once more it was the Finnish artillery which had imposed intolerable losses on the Russian infantry mass as it tried to cross the frozen river. The purpose of this Christmas massacre is difficult to guess, for the main offensive at Summa had failed already and there was no prospect of a decisive break-through on this sector. If the attacks on III Army Corps had been only diversionary, as seems most probable, they failed in this respect as well, since the Finnish 10 Division beat them off without calling for reinforcements.

Meretskov's main effort was at Summa and there the pattern of operations was different. The artillery preparation began on 16 December, and on 17 December the assault was led by tanks. These broke into and through the Finnish lines without much difficulty, and in the open terrain of the Summa sector could not easily be attacked in daylight – the Finnish anti-tank guns were not numerous or mobile enough and suffered serious losses. However, as long as the Finnish infantry stayed in their bunkers and dugouts, they were fairly safe from tanks, for the tank guns were not heavy enough to destroy them in these positions. So the tanks tended to cruise around and wait for the infantry to follow, but when these did appear, in the usual dense columns, they were easily dealt with. As night fell, the Finns emerged from their positions and hunted down the tanks – about twenty-five were destroyed in this manner out of sixty or seventy that had been committed. On the other hand, the Russian infantry used the cover of darkness to infiltrate some of the Finnish positions. The second day's fighting followed much the same lines – about seventy tanks attacked and were followed later by the infantry; another twenty-five tanks were destroyed, and infantry fell victims to the Finnish artillery and machine guns. After the defeat of a third attack on 19 December it was clear that the attempt to storm the Mannerheim line had failed: sporadic attacks continued until 22 December, but they had lost their force and were easily repulsed, while the Finnish positions were everywhere intact.

The battle had been a major victory for the Finns. The Russians had exerted their full strength and failed disastrously, without even forcing the Finns to use their reserves. Yet some of the more thoughtful Finnish commanders were disturbed at the ease with which the tanks had broken in; if they had been properly supported by their infantry and artillery the outcome might have been very different, and it had to be assumed that the Russians too would come to see this and act accordingly – as indeed they did. But the immediate reaction of the Finnish command was to see in the Russian defeat the opportunity for a counter-attack. Mannerheim agreed to release his strategic reserve, 6 Division, for a blow at what they supposed to be the shaken and demoralized Russians. Elements of five Finnish divisions would undertake an ambitious pincer movement, hoping either to trap substantial Russian forces, or at least to disrupt them. As speed was essential, before the Russians could recover, the attack was launched on the morning of 23 December, and it revealed that the Finnish army was not trained or equipped for such an operation. Because of the crude communication equipment they could not co-ordinate the movements of large forces on a broad front, nor bring their artillery to bear effectively when they ran up against resistance. But above all, the Finns had mis-judged the situation, for the Russians were not demoral-ized but had dug themselves in and fought back well. The Finns could recognize a failure when they met one, and the attack was broken off after some eight hours of fighting, but it had cost them about 1,500 casualties, and had been a nasty blow to army morale. It may, even so, have convinced the Russians that they faced a formidable enemy, and that to achieve results a completely new style of warfare was necessary: the signs are that they did realise this. The isthmus front virtually closed down until the end of January, with only patrol activity between the two sides. Thus by the end of December all the initial Russian attacks had been held, and the initiative had passed temporarily to the Finns. But before pursuing the story of how the Finnish command sought to exploit this situation, it is necessary to go back in time and trace the political developments.[8]

The capacity of the Finnish government for self-delusion had persisted to the end. On the morning of 30 November, when the first Russian bombs fell on Hel-sinki, the government was debating what Russia had meant by breaking off diplomatic relations, and even

[8] *Halsti*, pp. 166-7.

after the bombs had fallen some ministers would not face the fact that their policies had been based on a total miscalculation of Russian intentions. When the government met parliament on the evening of 30 November, Cajander would not recognise that a war had begun, but said 'our opponent has begun to pursue his aims with vigour', while Erkko claimed that 'it might yet be possible to avoid a situation in which Finland has to take arms in her defence'. But there was one leader, Tanner, who knew that this nonsense must stop. While he was sheltering from the first air-raid he told friends that Cajander and Erkko must be removed as a necessary precondition for the adoption of a realistic policy – by which he meant trying to end hostilities and resuming negotiation. He made sure of success that afternoon when he persuaded the socialist members of parliament to withdraw their ministers from the government. Then, as the leading ministers drove together to attend the parliamentary session in the evening, Tanner told Cajander that he must resign and consequently, although parliament gave the government a unanimous vote of confidence, it resigned immediately after.[9]

Tanner had also had a new prime minister in mind: Risto Ryti, the president of the Bank of Finland, a man of known moderation and well respected abroad. Ryti was, naturally, unenthusiastic about taking on a thankless mess that had been created by others, but the president of the republic, Kallio, pressed him hard, and Tanner offered to take up the key post of foreign minister. So, on 1 December, the new government took office. Apart from Ryti and Tanner, the most important change was the inclusion of Paasikivi, as minister without portfolio, in view of the negotiations which it was expected would begin. The new government met on 2 December and defined its two main policies as firstly to end hostilities and open talks as quickly as possible; and secondly to wage war with the utmost vigour in the meantime, to preserve a strong bargaining position. They got gloomy

[9] *Jakobson*, p. 158: *Tanner*, p. 91.

advice from Mannerheim to lose no time, as he did not anticipate that the front could be held for long.[10]

In the war-time government, effective power was concentrated in the hands of a small inner group, the quest for peace being handled by Tanner personally with the advice of Paasikivi, with Ryti being kept closely informed. The prosecution of the war was almost wholly in the care of Ryti, who handled it through his personal staff brought over from the Bank. Mannerheim kept in close touch through his personal liaison officer, General R. Walden, and at critical times, when Mannerheim had to be consulted personally, the ministers had to travel there for talks since he usually refused to leave headquarters. The president, Kallio, and the rest of the government played a secondary role in decision making. Their function was to ratify, often with the utmost reluctance, the policy decided on by the ruling clique. The first steps were taken on 2 December when it was decided to ask the Swedish government to act as mediator, and this was followed on 4 December by a request to Germany to lend her support to Sweden's effort. Parallel with this went measures to make effective resistance possible, which meant in effect looking for outside assistance. Again Sweden was the first power to be approached, and she was asked to agree to set up a joint Swedish-Finnish defence of the Åland islands; both parties knew the implications of this proposal, for if Sweden agreed she declared herself an ally of Finland in the war. The Swedish government recognized this, and only the foreign minister, Sandler, was prepared to agree to the Finnish request. When his colleagues insisted on sending a firm negative reply to Helsinki, Sandler resigned. The reply disappointed the Finns, as Paasikivi noted in his diary 'it made a depressing impact. It was taken to mean finally that no military assistance was to be expected from the Swedish government.' The Finns also decided to appeal to the League of Nations, partly in the hope that this might produce renewed diplomatic contact with the Soviet Union, but mainly because

[10] *Paasikivi*, pp. 118-9: *Jakobson*, pp. 160-1: *Tanner*, pp. 96-9.

an endorsement of the Finnish case by the League would put some moral pressure on members to help, and provide adequate legal grounds for those who were willing.[11]

The Council of the League met on 9 December to consider Finland's case and referred it to the Assembly two days later. The Assembly, after setting up a commission and hearing its report, resolved on 14 December that the Soviet Union had committed aggression and had refused to desist when asked, and that members of the League had a duty, therefore, to give Finland all the assistance they could – but it was significant how all the neighbours of the Soviet Union registered formal reservations and denied that the resolution was formally binding on them. The Council then met once more to consider the recommendation of the Assembly to expel the Soviet Union from membership, which was duly done, but with eight of the fifteen members declining to take part – the votes in favour were Britain, France, Belgium, South Africa, Egypt, Bolivia and the Dominican Republic. The significance of this combination speaks for itself. It is tempting to dismiss this last action of the League of Nations as the fitting conclusion to the history of a deeply flawed organization, yet it had its value for Finland. For one thing, as the theoretical voice of world opinion the League resolution gave a great boost to Finnish morale – they felt they were not alone in their struggle. Secondly, as Paasikivi noted, 'for us the decision of the League of Nations had the value that both Finland and the nations who sought to help her could appeal to it', and it will be seen that eventually some of them did.[12]

The effort to reopen negotiations with Russia through a mediator were doomed to failure, and the cause was the emergence of the Finnish Peoples' government under the chairmanship of the exiled communist, O. W. Kuusinen. It will be recalled that this institution had been a basic feature of the original Russian plan. This govern-

[11] *Paasikivi*, p. 122.
[12] *Paasikivi*, p. 128.

ment was announced on 30 November and identified on
1 December as being located in the Finnish border town
of Terijoki, and it was at once recognized by the Soviet
Union as the real government of Finland. The theory
was that the Finnish Communist party, together with
other unspecified democratic elements, had overthrown
the capitalist government of Finland and replaced it with
this new government which expressed the true aspirations of the overwhelming majority of Finnish people.
The public statements of the Kuusinen government
stressed that this was not a communist revolution, and
that Finland was not to adopt the Soviet system, for
which she was not yet ready. Instead the government
suggested a programme of radical reform which was to
be submitted to the decision of a free Finnish parliament as a basis for discussion. It was emphasized that
there was no question of the sovereign independence of
the Finnish republic being undermined. The government, and the army which it claimed to control, were
depicted as leading a popular mass movement in a
struggle with the Finnish reactionaries, who had tried to
drag Finland into an imperialist adventure against the
Soviet Union. The government solemnly appealed to the
Soviet Union to help it in this struggle and the appeal
was favourably received. On 2 December, Kuusinen, on
behalf of his government, signed a mutual assistance
treaty which ceded to Russia all she had asked for in
October, but in return the whole of Soviet Karelia was
to be united with the new People's Republic of Finland.
The two governments were stated to be in process of
'liquidating the actual seat of war which the former
plutocratic government had created on behalf of the
imperialist powers on the borders of the Soviet Union.'[13]

In this way Russia defined her war-aims. In one respect
these had not changed since October; Russia still sought
an agreement of limited scope with an independent Finland, and guaranteed that she did not seek to annex or
'Sovietise' the country, but now the aims of October were

[13] *Mannerheim*, pp. 141-5.

74

to be further secured by the installation of a Finnish government that could be relied on to work closely with the Soviet Union. In fact the plan, as revealed by Kuusinen to his colleagues, was to broaden the Kuusinen government into some kind of broad radical coalition once they were installed in Helsinki. Kuusinen's colleagues were told that they were to regard their offices as provisional only.[14]

This scenario for the Finnish People's government was almost wholly fictitious; in reality it was an embryo puppet régime created to give some kind of propaganda justification for the Russian aggression against Finland. It turned out to be a tragic error. In the first place, the government was a farce. Its members did indeed sit in Terijoki, but they had nothing to govern and little to do except draft propaganda material for use by the Russians; the 'army' consisted of a few thousand conscripted Finnish exiles, who were put into distinctive uniforms, and originally intended for show purposes only – they would provide some kind of initial security force for the new régime once the fighting was over. It is unclear whether in the end this force was ever sent into action. But the real weakness of the scheme was the fact that the Kuusinen government evoked no response inside Finland except contempt. This was partly because the Finnish authorities had rounded up all the native communists and put them into prison camps; and partly because in the circumstances in which it was set up the government had had no opportunity to establish any kind of contacts inside Finland. But chiefly it suffered because, as a government of Finland, it lacked all credibility; with the exception of Kuusinen himself, all the members were obscure party hacks, for all the known and prestigious party leaders had been liquidated in the Stalin purges. So that even the Finnish workers, the Kuusinen government was a sick joke and in the world at large it was immediately recognized for what it was – a crude deception. Yet this pathetic charade had an immense influence

[14] *Tuominen*, p. 62.

on the war, and thousands died uselessly because of it. The reason for this emerges in Molotov's reply to the Swedish offer of mediation, and in the replies to the League of Nations. Molotov told the League secretary that 'the Soviet Union is not at war with Finland and does not threaten the Finnish people. The Soviet Union maintains peaceful relations with the Democratic Republic of Finland. The people in whose name Holsti appeals to the League are not the real representatives of the people of Finland.' Thus the Russian contention was that Finland had only one legitimate government, the Finnish Peoples' government, and that mediation was irrelevant because the Soviet Union had no dispute with Finland – on the contrary she enjoyed excellent relations with the real Finnish government. The thinking behind the Russian plan was revealed by Molotov in a conversation with the German ambassador on 4 December. He said that the war would be over very soon, the People's government would establish its authority, and the whole unfortunate business quickly wound up. Thus the attempts of the government in Helsinki to reopen negotiations with Russia were blocked by the existence of Kuusinen's government. After the Swedish government had been rebuffed in Moscow on 4 December, the Finns continued to hope that contact might be re-established, and as late as 15 December Tanner made an offer over the radio to resume negotiations, but the Soviet government rejected his effort with contempt – for the moment they were publicly and inescapably committed to Kuusinen.[15]

This left the Finns with no choice but to fight on and hope that something would turn up, which could only mean enlisting some kind of outside help. Sweden remained the most obvious source, and despite her refusal to join in the defence of Åland, the Finnish leaders did not give up hope. They knew that the war had produced a wave of pro-Finnish feeling in Sweden, led by activists like Sandler, and this might be exploited in order to

[15] *Tuominen*, p. 64: *Paasikivi*, p. 125: *DGFP*, p. 487.

force the hand of the government. But the activists were out-manoeuvred by the prime minister, Hansson, who met the danger by forming a national coalition government on 13 December, which included all parties, and had a programme which, while offering all aid short of war to the Finnish cause, clearly ruled out actual military participation. This move deprived those elements in Sweden who favoured intervention of any organized political leadership, and reduced Sandler and his friends to a group of isolated individuals. Paasikivi noted in his diary on 14 December that the new government's statement on Finland was 'dry and saddening'. The official Swedish position was, and remained to the end, that they would do anything to facilitate a resumption of negotiations between Finland and Russia. In the meantime they would send military and civil supplies to Finland, permit Swedish citizens to organize assistance and volunteer as individuals for service in Finland, including active members of the armed forces, and they would permit other nations to send supplies and individual volunteers through Swedish territory – but beyond that they would not go.[16]

The official reasons for this attitude, as embodied in numerous responses to pressure from the Finnish government, rested on two assertions: that Swedish public opinion was firm in adhering to neutrality and the avoidance of conflict with a great power; and that if Sweden did intervene, she would be subjected to counter action by Germany. The first of these was probably true as far as it goes, although if the Swedish government had given a lead in favour of intervention public opinion might have responded. The second amounted to a bare-faced lie: the Swedish government was naturally apprehensive about what Germany might do if Sweden offered armed support to Finland, and it therefore had a duty to find out before committing itself. But all the enquiries that were made of the Germans on this point, from Hitler in person downwards, elicited the same response – that if

16 *Paasikivi*, p. 138.

Sweden acted by herself, Germany would be indifferent and would not intervene. The reality was that the Swedish government had determined, as a cold-blooded calculation, that Sweden had more to lose by becoming embroiled in a war with Russia than she had by a Russian conquest of Finland, however unpleasant that might be. The talk put out by the Swedish government about German pressures was to disguise the ugly truth that in the last resort, and in order to save her own skin, Sweden would leave Finland to perish.[17]

Germany was the only other nation in a position to intervene directly in the Russo-Finnish war, and it was very difficult for the Finns to understand why she would not play her natural role in the Baltic area. The German government's (more properly, Hitler's) position was clear and consistent. As long as the war in the west continued Germany would do nothing to endanger her collaboration with Soviet Russia. Germany was inconvenienced by the Russian attack on Finland, and when later it threatened to lead to serious complications in Scandinavia by providing an excuse for an Anglo-French intervention, the Germans faced real danger. So she always wanted the war to end, but she would not put any pressure on the Soviet Union to bring this about. There was pressure inside Germany favourable to Finland, one source of which was the German ambassador in Helsinki, Blücher, who kept up a stream of pained protests at the way in which Finnish good-will towards Germany was being squandered. Hitler, however, was adamant. On 2 December all German diplomats were instructed to avoid any utterance that could be interpreted as anti-Russian, and this was reinforced by a circular from von Ribbentrop himself on 7 December. When Russia enquired about the possibility of German ships fuelling Russian submarines in the Baltic, Hitler at once agreed in principle, though the freezing of the Baltic meant that nothing came out of it. Germany refused to let her Italian ally send war material to Finland through Germany, and

[17] *DGFP*, pp. 297, 862.

when Finnish emissaries persuaded Göring, on 18 December, to accept a scheme for secret sales of German arms to Finland under elaborate cover, Hitler vetoed the plan. All this made Germany the one country in the world whose neutrality was clearly biased in favour of Russia. As the head of the German foreign office told Blücher on 1 January 1940, Germany's international position did not permit the slightest equivocation in her dealings with the Soviet Union.[18]

It has been shown that the main British interest in the Russo-Finnish conflict lay initially in the possibility that it would lead to conflict between Germany and Russia, through their Baltic rivalry. Thus, although Halifax declared Britain's support for Finland on 30 November, and after considerable hesitation agreed that Britain would vote for Finland's case in the League of Nations, the basic British position was that recommended by the chiefs-of-staff and endorsed by the cabinet in November – that a Russian invasion of Finland was no threat to Allied interests, and that in any case the Allies could not offer any effective help. Only if the Russian action extended to Sweden and Norway would intervention be considered. This British attitude was virtually binding on France as well, because only Britain could provide the facilities for mounting any kind of intervention in Scandinavia. On 3 December, after the war had begun, Chamberlain wrote, 'I don't think the Allied cause is likely to suffer'. All this added up to a situation in which there was no prospect of any direct military intervention on Finland's behalf.[19]

However, the League of Nations resolution, combined with almost world-wide feeling in favour of Finland, did produce some material assistance. Funds were raised in several countries on Finland's behalf, notably in the USA and Sweden, and governments provided credit facilities

---

[18] *DGFP*, pp. 267, 319, 479, 501, 507, 511, 521, 596.
[19] *Woodward*, pp. 38, 41: K. Feiling, *Life of Neville Chamberlain*, p. 427: G. A. Gripenberg, *Finland and the Great Powers*, p. 88. (Hereafter *Gripenberg*).

for Finnish purchases, and helped by releasing war materials for sale. In addition quantities of food, clothing, medical supplies and raw materials were either given or sold on credit. There was, however, a major logistic problem. Since Germany would not allow transit across the territory she controlled, and the Russians had closed off Petsamo, the only access to Finland was by way of Norway. All relief had to be sent to Norwegian ports, using the Allied convoy system, which by itself imposed considerable delays. Then the goods had to be sent on by rail to the Finnish frontier, and trans-shipped there because Finnish railways had a different gauge. It took a month, on average, for a shipment to get from the factory or depot to the Finnish border, and considerable extra time before military equipment could be sorted, made ready and put into the hands of the troops. Even aircraft, with few exceptions, were sent crated by sea and rail, and had to be assembled in Finland on arrival. The only supplies exempted from these delays were those from Sweden. They were the most valuable, precisely because they arrived in time to be used. The Swedish government gave various kinds of assistance, and private subscription provided more. Most important was the release of weapons from Swedish stocks for purchase by Finland or on loan; the 80,000 rifles, eighty-five anti-tank guns, 104 anti-aircraft guns, 112 field guns and ammunition for these, which were supplied through the Swedish government, were the most valuable material assistance that Finland received.

The other major suppliers were Britain and France, but they had special problems of their own, the most obvious being that they needed their modern equipment for their armed forces. In addition it was Allied policy at this time to give priority to Turkey and the Balkans in distributing what surplus equipment was available. Even so, Britain supplied over 100 aircraft of reasonably modern type, and both allies provided quantities of small arms, mines, artillery and ammunition, some of which was a gift, the rest was supplied on credit. But the two weapons that the Finns needed most urgently, anti-tank and anti-aircraft guns, were the types that France and Britain were least able to supply. Finland did receive some aircraft and artillery from the United States, and other war material came from Italy, Spain, Hungary and Belgium. It is very difficult to evaluate this aid, for there are no accurate estimates of how much of it actually reached the fighting front before the end of hostilities; it is known that substantial quantities were still in Norwegian harbours when the Germans invaded that country in April. Further, not all the weapons that did arrive could be used effectively. Crews had to be trained to use unfamiliar weapons and aircraft, some of the equipment was really obsolete and of doubtful value, while the proliferation of varying types of weapon and different calibres of ammunition was always a nuisance and could be a menace. It can only be said that, excluding the Swedish assistance, which was in a class of its own, the material aid that was given cannot have harmed the Finnish war effort, and in some areas, as when it boosted the inadequate domestic production of ammunition, was very valuable. There was, however, one other significant source of outside supply. In the course of the battles on the eastern front, soon to be described, the Finns captured significant quantities of useable motor transport, guns and ammunition, some of which was put into service straight away. The diary of a Russian officer noted bitterly how his position was being shelled by a four-gun 122-mm battery which the Finns had just captured from his division. Some of this booty, like the captured tanks, was of no immediate use except as a morale booster, but to an army as desperately short of all kinds of equipment as the Finns, the rest was very welcome.[20]

The other possible kind of aid to Finland was manpower. There were the same difficulties to be faced in getting the actual volunteers into Finland and, having got them there, forming them into viable military units.

[20] *Lehmus,* p. 79.

Most governments were willing to allow enlistments, and voluntary organizations in the various countries handled the actual recruiting. For instance, in Britain, the government gave permission to enlist men for Finland in January, and by the first week in March a hundred men were ready to leave; but the war was over by the time they arrived, while the numbers involved indicate that this kind of private recruitment could only have token significance. In reality the volunteer movement had no material impact on the war. Once more Sweden provided the exception, and for the same reasons of proximity, allied with the willingness of the Swedish government to release serving soldiers and allow them to take their personal weapons with them. This allowed two battalions of Swedes to go into action in the very last days of the war – the only foreigners to do so, apart from isolated individuals.

It is therefore a temptation to write off the outside assistance given to Finland as of no real value – too little and too late – and Finnish writers tend to do this. They emphasise, with grudging acknowledgement of the Swedish contribution, that Finland fought alone and owed nothing significant to foreign help. If this contention is judged in terms of actual manpower and military hardware delivered to the front, it has a great deal of validity. But it overlooks the extent to which the foreign aid movement boosted Finnish morale, particularly on the home front – the Finns believed that most of the world was on their side and that in theory they were not alone in the struggle against impossible odds. There is no way of calculating what this factor was worth in keeping the Finns going and in masking from the ordinary citizen the brutal truth that they were isolated in their struggle. The declared support of the civilized world seemed to give some ground for the belief that the fight was worth maintaining because the world would not let Finland's cause go down to defeat in the long run.

When the fighting died down on the isthmus in December, the military side of the war entered a new phase, in which the interest focused on the eastern front, where the initiative had passed to the Finns. This phase produced a series of remarkable operations, all based on a common situation: a Russian invading column, road-bound and experiencing difficulty with supplies and the severe climate, had been halted and reduced to passivity by the Finns. It was then open to the Finnish command to use the mobility of its troops across country to strike at the flank and rear of these Russian columns and destroy them, since they were so immobilized they could not even retreat. The strategic aim of the Finnish command in these battles was to eliminate the invaders along the whole length of the eastern front, and to release the bulk of the Finnish forces involved for service on the isthmus front. If this aim had been achieved, the equivalent of three divisions of high quality troops would have become available. But this strategy failed on the whole, in spite of brilliant tactical successes, because the Russians, instead of breaking up under attack, tended to congeal into hedgehog positions, which the Finns called *mottis*. These could only have been reduced quickly if the Finns had had adequate artillery and air power, which they did not. The Russians were able to supply the larger *mottis* from the air adequately enough to keep them fighting, while the Finns were driven into tactics of slow attrition, which sufficed to reduce the smaller *mottis*, but could not break down the big ones. So the strategic aims of these Finnish attacks were frustrated, and all their forces on the eastern front were still fully tied down there at the end of the war.

The most important of the sectors of the eastern front was that of IV Army Corps, which had halted the Russian 168 and 18 divisions on the line Kitelä-Syskyjärvi. The sector was vital because any Russian break-through here would expose the rear of the troops fighting on the isthmus and make their positions untenable. Hägglund's command had never intended that, once the Russians had been halted they should be left alone, but had planned from the first to eliminate them by a counter-attack. The pre-condition for this was that the Finnish left-flank position at Kollaa could be held without needing reinforcement. Fortunately the troops at Kollaa, four battalions of infantry and a little artillery, did manage to hold back two Russian divisions: as long as the Russians were confined to the road they could not deploy to any effect, and their repeated attacks on the Kollaa position failed. By 18 December they gave up and lapsed into positional warfare, and did not renew the assault until March when they were again beaten back. The Kollaa position was substantially intact at the end of the war, yet in all this time only one regiment of Finnish reinforcements had been drawn into the battle. Thus the offensive plans of IV Army Corps could proceed.

The Finnish troops had to learn the art of this kind of warfare through hard experience: the first attempt of IV Army Corps at a flanking movement (on 12 December) failed because it was over-ambitious. The attacking column made a long sweep across country which brought the troops into action physically exhausted, and with their heavy equipment lagging in the rear. The second attempt, on 17 December, failed because it did not take a wide enough sweep – the Russians were able to switch their reserves to meet it. Before the third and decisive effort the climate intervened to help the Finns; there was a sharp drop in temperature and a heavy snowfall which further reduced Russian mobility, but helped the movement of ski troops. The next phase began on 27 December and built up to a climax on 5 January, when the Finns swept round and through the Russian 18 Division and cut both the supply roads which led back across the frontier. This should have led to the rapid destruction of the two enemy divisions, but instead *motti* warfare set in. 18 Division was cut up into numerous isolated pockets, each of which dug in and held fast; 168 Division congealed into one big *motti* on the shore of Lake Ladoga at Kitelä. The Russians showed some ingenuity in constructing these positions; often rings of tanks were dug in deep and were virtually impervious to Finnish

artillery fire. The Finns found themselves cheated of
the expected victory, as each *motti* had to be reduced
by attrition. Wherever the Russians were foolish enough
to try and break out, the Finnish ski troops destroyed
them on the move; where a *motti* was long and narrow
it could be chopped into sections and wiped out piece
by piece; where it was consolidated and well positioned
even a small *motti* had great staying power. This was
demonstrated by the fate of 18 Division. It was eventually
destroyed and most of its equipment, including 100 tanks,
fell to the Finns, but it was 29 February before the last
motti was liquidated. The Kitelä *motti* could not be
reduced; it was big enough in area to be supplied from
the air and in the end, on 6 March, Russian forces attacking over the frozen lake re-opened direct contact with
it.

Captured Russian diaries reflect both the horrors of
life within the *motti* and the residual toughness which
enabled the defenders to hang on. One such, from a
motti of 18 Division, described the major hazard as
Finnish snipers; whenever the defenders had to leave
their dugouts to collect supplies they suffered casualties.
Once they had eaten the horses, food began to run out.
The air drops often fell in enemy lines, and were in any
case irregular; by 25 February the men had been
unfed for two days, and discipline wavered. When packages fell within range, the men 'run like maniacs, they
tear at the packages, eat and die. Food is all in all to
them. And a hungry human is an animal.' Yet when
they were attacked they defended their positions successfully, for they could hear the artillery fire of relieving
forces, and the diarist's own faith in victory was un-
shaken, 'We do not lose hope. We shall certainly win.
There is no doubt of that, nothing else is possible.' The
Finns were facing a toughness which, in its way, was
equal to their own and baulked them of the fruits of
victory which should have followed a successful encirclement. Thus it was that on 13 March, when the
fighting ended, IV Army Corps, in spite of brilliant

successes, was still tied down north of Lake Ladoga.[21]

Next to IV Army Corps, proceeding northwards, was the command of Colonel Talvela, which had blocked the advance of the Russian 139 Division at Tolvajärvi and was holding off 155 Division at Ilomantsi. On 12 December, Talvela struck at 139 division, and although his flanking movement failed, a Finnish frontal attack, delivered by infantry across the open terrain of a frozen lake and against Russians dug in with armoured support, succeeded. In three days of fierce fighting 139 Division broke up and was destroyed, though a simultaneous attack on 155 Division made no headway. As Talvela pursued the fleeing survivors of 139 Division along the road back to the frontier, he ran into the Russian 75 Division at Ägläjärvi. This division in turn was outflanked, for it dared not leave the road, and threatened with encirclement until it retired in disorder to Aittojoki, where the Finnish advance stopped. If the Finns had had some fresh troops, or adequate artillery, they could have broken this position too, and threatened the rear of the Russian forces at Kollaa, but Talvela's men had exhausted their offensive capacity. This was shown in their operations against 155 Division, for although they kept it immobile near Ilomantsi, it could not be shifted or destroyed. Even so, Talvela's command had destroyed one Russian division and badly mauled a second. Their booty included sixty tanks, thirty guns and over 400 automatic weapons, and was the first major haul of captured material to become available for equipping the Finns' own troops. Further, Tolvajärvi was the first decisive offensive victory won by the Finnish army and had an enormous effect on morale.

But the greatest of the Finnish victories was won by Colonel Siilasvuo at Suomussalmi. Siilasvuo commanded the Finnish 9 Brigade, which was only partly equipped and had no anti-tank guns, facing the Russian 163 Division. The village of Suomussalmi was at the junction

[21] *Lehmus,* pp. 80, 85, 86.

of two roads coming from the frontier, a northern road from Juntusranta and a southern road from Raate. Siilasvuo began well by cutting the Raate road behind the Russians on 11 December, and moved up it towards Suomussalmi from the east. The Russians there did not think of retiring, for they knew, and the Finns did not, that a new Russian division, 44 Division, was advancing to their relief from Raate. The Finns pressed their attack on Suomussalmi, though badly troubled by tanks, and on 22 December Mannerheim raised Siilasvuo's command to a division by sending two further regiments of replacement troops. While Siilasvuo prepared to use these for his decisive blow, his men cut the northern road on 27 December and the following day 163 Division broke up, leaving eleven tanks, twenty-five guns and some 500 prisoners in Finnish hands. The stragglers who tried to flee across the wilderness fell victim to the savage cold and Finnish ski patrols.

163 Division was destroyed because the expected support from 44 Division did not come. There is indeed a mystery about the behaviour of this unit, for its commanders were informed by radio of the plight of 163 Division and yet, instead of pushing forward, they halted and dug in along the Raate road. Further, they did this in the worst possible way, with the division strung out in a thin line along the road for several kilometres. Siilasvuo turned on 44 Division on 2 January, attacking in the classic manner of this kind of operation. The Finns launched unceasing raids from the forest, through which they could move their men at will parallel to the road. Where the Russian tanks were active, the Finns had to stay in the shelter of the trees, but soon they had both ends of the Russian column blocked off and proceeded to harass it unmercifully from both flanks. By 6 January the fight was almost over; 44 Division broke up and small groups tried to get away through the forest. The Finns took thirty-five tanks, fifty guns and the whole of the division's heavy equipment. This time the Finns had won a full strategic victory, for with the destruction

of these two divisions Russian activity on this sector came to an end, and Siilasvuo's division became free for use elsewhere.

Mannerheim now had a whole division at his disposal and he decided to use it for a repeat performance against the Russian 54 Division at Kuhmo. Siilasvuo received orders to move his troops to the new front on 18 January, and was ready to begin operations on 26 January. The situation at Kuhmo was not quite the same as at Suomussalmi. It was true the Russian division was spread along a road, but it had been virtually unmolested for some weeks, and the men were dug in in wooden bunkers strong enough to resist mortars and light artillery, which was all that Siilasvuo had got. Further, the Russians had made an air-strip on a frozen lake for landing their supplies. Siilasvuo himself says that he judged in advance that his force was too weak for its assignment – there was not enough artillery, and what there was was short of ammunition – but he did his best.

The Finnish 9 Division was at its full strength of three regiments, and joined the covering forces which had kept 54 Division under observation. The Finns took time to set up supply routes and depots and a camp of heated tents for the attacking force to operate from, although Russian air activity confined them to the hours of darkness. One improvement for 9 Division was that they had the Russian anti-tank guns captured at Suomussalmi, which proved very effective against 54 Division's attempts to use its armour in the near vicinity of the road. The Finnish offensive began on 28 January and soon won its initial objectives – the road back was cut in the rear of the Russians, and they were split into three *mottis* by flanking attacks. It then became apparent, however, that the Finns were simply not strong enough to finish the job. 54 Division did not break up but maintained an active defence, while supplies from the air frustrated the effects of blockade. In addition, the Finnish efforts were distracted by two major relief attempts. One was by the Russian 23 Division which tried to break through from the east by road, and although it was held off the effort drew in considerable Finnish resources. The other was a spectacular relief attempt by a Russian ski brigade under Colonel Dolin, mounted across country. The presence of this force became known to the Finns on 10 February, and was the biggest Russian attempt of the war to emulate the Finnish use of ski troops. It became clear that the Russians were inadequately trained and equipped. They did surprise and overrun a Finnish transport column, but their own headquarters was ambushed by a Finnish patrol, and a similar fate overtook most of the rest of the brigade; it became scattered and was hunted down in small groups. One such group was cornered in some wooden huts and preferred death in the flames to surrender – only four prisoners were taken out of over 300 men. In this way Dolin's brigade was annihilated in a three-day hunt over the wilderness, and showed they were no match for the Finns at this type of warfare. For instance their weapons were not properly protected against frost, and on several occasions the Russians were unable to shoot. Even so, Siilasvuo had to detach valuable forces to deal with the intruders, and this further weakened the attack on 54 Division; indeed the Finns were lucky that the division made no effort to co-operate with the relieving force, but remained passive while the Finns dealt with it. In the end, although Siilasvuo nibbled away at the *mottis* of 54 Division, they were still fighting when the war ended, so that 9 Division was wholly tied down.

It could be argued that on balance the operations against 54 Division represented a Finnish failure, for while the Russians could afford the losses they suffered, Mannerheim urgently needed 9 Division for more important tasks. With the advantage of hindsight it can be seen that the Russians at Kuhmo were doing no harm and could well have been left there. On the other hand, 23 Division was approaching from across the frontier, and perhaps the Finnish command would have had to commit some troops to this sector in the end. The

Kuhmo fighting certainly showed that victories like Tolvajärvi and Suomussalmi could not be produced to order; a combination of specially favourable circumstances and reasonable luck was needed. Where the Russians kept their nerve, stayed put and dug in solidly they had a fighting chance of survival. This was demonstrated in the last and most northerly of these offensive operations, against the Russian 122 Division in the Salla sector. In this case the Finns had only one infantry regiment and a collection of small miscellaneous units, and these were simply not strong enough: it proved easy enough to get round behind the Russians and harass their communications, driving them into fortified positions along the road, but two attempts on 2 January and 19 January to compel 122 Division to retreat were abortive. On 26 February a Swedish volunteer battalion took over this sector and released the bulk of the Finnish force for use in the final, decisive battles round Viipuri.

Any general assessment of these battles on the eastern front must first recognize that the Finnish offensives were remarkable and tactically brilliant feats of arms, but then admit that strategically they failed. It can be assumed that if the Finns had possessed a few more troops, or had had adequate artillery and air support, they could have achieved strategic victory too and closed down the eastern front – but that would have needed a Suomussalmi in every sector, and this was beyond their power. From a military point of view the result of the fighting was a stalemate: the Russian threat on the eastern front was halted, if not eliminated, but almost all the Finnish forces had to stay there until the end of the war. The outcome of the war was affected only in a negative way; the Russians could not break in on the rear of the Finnish troops defending the Karelian isthmus, but they were able to fight that battle without any fear of intervention from the Finnish forces on the eastern front. On the other hand, these battles had two political consequences of the utmost importance. First, although the Finnish command knew that the victories

were incomplete, the Finnish public and the government gained the false impression that the war was being
won. Paasikivi was one of the few civilian leaders who
was able to see these successes in their right perspective.
He wrote in his diary on 8 January, 'our victories are
considered tremendously great, and from our point of
view they are magnificent, but they have no effect on
the final result, since in view of the power of the huge
Russian state, these defeats have no significance.' Most
of the civilians accepted the victories at their face value,
and it will be shown how this led them into serious political miscalculations. But the second consequence was
much graver and was to affect the history of the whole
western world, for it was these Russian disasters which
created the delusion that the Red Army was not to be
taken seriously as a fighting force. While the incompetence and its appalling results in terms of Russian losses
were clear enough to outside observers, the special circumstances of this campaign in a sub-arctic forest wilderness, in the depth of the coldest winter of the century
were not taken sufficiently into account. The general misreading of these battles first led the Allies to the brink
of an adventure that could have involved them in war
with the Soviet Union (because they had come to think
of Russia as militarily a negligible quantity), and then
helped to lead Hitler to make those miscalculations which
doomed his Russian campaign to defeat in 1941.[22]

[22] *Paasikivi*, p. 146.

IV

The Russo-Finnish War, Phase Two
The Russian Victory

It will be shown that the Russians had no thought of accepting defeat and that their first reaction was to plan for a second attempt; at the same time they were sufficiently impressed by the toughness of Finnish resistance to change their political aims in the course of January. Tanner had never abandoned hope of getting in touch with Moscow and re-opening negotiations. There had been soundings through Estonia in December which suggested that Russia was ready to talk, but the terms would be as before and there would have to be a different Finnish government – and since no one on the Finnish side was willing to negotiate on this basis nothing came of it. Then in January two new initiatives were launched. On 1 January the Finnish playwright, H. Wuolijoki, wrote to Tanner and offered to go to Stockholm and talk to her old friend the Russian ambassador, Mme A. Kollontai. Tanner was very sceptical because he regarded Mme Wuolijoki as both silly and unreliable, but he discussed it with Paasikivi and Ryti and they urged that Wuolijoki be allowed to try; she therefore left for Stockholm on 10 January. Meanwhile, Tanner tried an alternative approach through Germany. Blücher was invited for a talk on 4 January, and Tanner let fall a query whether Germany had any suggestion about how peace might be procured. Tanner quickened Blücher's interest by hinting that if Germany could not help, Finland would be driven to appeal to Britain and France. This was immediately reported back to Berlin, and some investigations were made. On 8 January, Schulenburg reported a conversation with Molotov, who had conceded that things were going badly in Finland, and when the ambassador suggested that Helsinki was ready for renewed talks 'Molotov did not, interestingly enough, make an entirely negative reply but answered with the words that it was "late, very late" for this.' The matter was considered in Berlin at the highest level, but in the end, on 17 January, Blücher was told that Germany saw no prospect of helping to end the conflict, and Schulenburg was told the same. It was clear that Hitler had decided against trying. Blücher duly reported his government's attitude to Tanner, and the Finns accepted that for the present this channel was closed. Confirmation was secured by Paasikivi, who wrote to his old German colleague, General von der Goltz, who in turn approached Hitler directly and was given to understand that although Germany naturally wanted to see the war ended, the Russians insisted on recognizing only Kuusinen's government, and therefore no fruitful mediation was possible.[1]

By the time that Paasikivi got his answer, on 3 February, the Finnish leaders knew that Russian policy had changed. Wuolijoki had been well received by Mme Kollontai in Stockholm, and Moscow had responded to the contact by sending out two foreign ministry officials to investigate. Once the Russians were satisfied that Finland was serious in desiring to resume negotiations, they hinted to the Swedish government that a new offer of mediation would be acceptable, and a Swedish note agreeing to this role was sent off on 25 January. It is interesting to try and fix the point at which the Soviet leadership decided to sacrifice the Kuusinen government as the price for getting peace negotiations started. When Molotov spoke to Schulenburg on 25 January he insisted that, at most, the Kuusinen government could be broadened and peace concluded with the 'democratic Finnish government' which would result. This must have been a deception designed to exclude Germany from claiming any share in the peace making; the Russians were at all times careful not to open any possibility of German interference, which was one reason why

---

[1] *DGFP*, pp. 613, 631, 644, 677: *Tanner*, pp. 123-4: *Paasikivi*, p.139.

they tried to ensure that Sweden should be the sole intermediary. The Soviet policy change must have happened about this point, for on 29 January the Russian government sent an official reply to Sweden accepting the offer of mediation. This reply, which marks the major turning point of the war, began: 'The Soviet Union has no objection in principle to concluding an agreement with the Ryti-Tanner government' and went on to say that Finland must suggest terms. But the Soviet Union would require more than she had demanded in October, 'because since those negotiations blood has been shed on both sides and that blood, which has been shed contrary to our hopes and through no fault of ours, calls for augmented guarantees of the security of the frontiers of the Soviet Union.'[2]

This note should have made the position clear, though it was fogged by a gloss from Mme Kollantai, transmitted privately through Wuolijoki, hinting that in fact Russia might still offer compensation, either territorial or economic, if her demands were met, and that later on, when the international situation improved, Finland might be allowed to seek modification of the terms. This gloss was either sheer invention on Kollontai's part, or a deliberate bait to delude Finland and Sweden into thinking that real bargaining was possible. In fact the Russian position left no room for manoeuvre: they wanted at least what had been demanded in October and would give nothing in return.

In spite of this, the Russian note of 29 January meant that Finland's fight had won her one major victory, for once the Soviet Union agreed to negotiate with the real Finnish government, the country's continuing independence was no longer in question. One can only speculate as to why the Soviet leadership was ready to accept this humiliating defeat, and prepared to sacrifice the puppet government which they had made the centre-piece of their policy. It was not military failure alone, for it will be seen that they had already taken measures which they

[2] *DGFP*, p. 708: *Tanner*, p. 126: *Jakobson*, p. 210.

could confidently expect to produce a military solution in the end, but on the other hand they now knew by experience that the Finnish army was not to be trifled with, and had to reckon that it might take some considerable time and much hard fighting before the result was certain. Then there is the possibility that Stalin had originally been persuaded into supporting the Kuusinen government against his better judgement, only because his policy of negotiating with Finland had been frustrated. He could see by January that the whole policy had been a blunder and wanted to cut his losses – in effect he had reverted to his original plan as soon as he saw a real chance to resume the talks.

One factor that is well established is that the Finnish war had developed far beyond the original Russian intentions. Conceived as a brief side-show to be handled by the Leningrad military district, it had become a major campaign with adverse consequences that were becoming increasingly obvious. Schulenburg had reported on 8 January that 'the war against Finland was from the very beginning unpopular with the people of the Soviet Union . . . This sentiment is strengthened by the absence of victories, increasing supply difficulties . . . the large number of Red Army soldiers with frozen limbs who are crowding the provincial hospitals.' It is unlikely that Stalin was swayed much by public opinion, but the disruption being caused by the military effort against Finland was another matter. The campaigning season in Europe was about to open, Stalin had interests in the Balkans which he wished to pursue, and he could not afford to have so many of his best troops bogged down in Finland. Finally, the Soviet government was acutely aware of a new and growing menace – that of Anglo-French intervention. It will be seen that this was no imaginary danger and that plans did exist which included the possibility of attacks on Russia's oilfields in the Caucasus as well as sending troops into Finland. Norway and Sweden had been warned in Russian notes of 5 and 6 January not to lend themselves to any such

Anglo-French schemes, and Molotov admitted to Schulenburg on 8 January that Russia was concerned, 'the Soviet government was aware of the danger that would arise if England and France should use Norway and Sweden for their own ends.' There are strong grounds for supposing that this danger was a major incentive for seeking a quick end to the war, and that the combination of all these factors must have looked compelling in the eyes of the Soviet leaders. Yet they could not make peace at any price: the terms must show, by the concessions extracted from Finland, that she acknowledged defeat, otherwise the Soviet Union would lose all credibility as a great power.[3]

On 30 January, Ryti, Tanner and Paasikivi met to decide how to respond to the Russian note, and it became apparent that the first two had been influenced by the illusion of military success. Indeed, Ryti had been fortified by a recent interview with Mannerheim, in which the commander-in-chief told him the current military situation was tolerable and did not compel the making of peace on unfavourable terms; in particular there was no need to concede a base on the Gulf of Finland. Thus, although Paasikivi pressed for a realistic reply to the Russians, Ryti and Tanner felt that they could afford to answer in general terms and suggest that the Finnish negotiating position of October could be taken as the basis of discussions. The Finnish reply said only that 'since common ground can only be reached by way of compromise, the position arrived at in the Moscow talks could in general be taken as a starting point. Besides Finland is prepared to make additional concessions which could be held necesary for the security of Leningrad.' The only specific suggestions were the surrender of more territory on the isthmus and the neutralization of the Gulf of Finland, and for this Finland would require compensation in territory and cash. This reply, which is based on the assumption that Russia would acknowledge military defeat and settle for terms close to those she

[3] *DGFP*, p. 629.

had already rejected in October, was not realistic in terms of Molotov's note; and by the time it had been sent to the Swedish government, this had been made clearer by a further Russian note which stated that the granting of a base at Hanko was a precondition for talks.[4]

Wuolijoki now suggested that perhaps Tanner himself should come to Stockholm and meet madame Kollontai for direct negotiation, and when this was agreed, a rendezvous was arranged, in the greatest secrecy, in the Grand Hotel in Stockholm. It was soon apparent that the base at Hanko was the key issue, and Tanner took it on himself to suggest that Finland might concede an island for a base if suitable territorial compensation were offered. He had no authority to do this, but could see that something would have to be offered to get talks started. Tanner and Kollontai had a second meeting on 6 February, and Tanner was given the official Soviet reply to the Finnish note: 'We regret that the proposal does not offer a sufficient basis for negotiations.' Tanner tried to keep the exchange going and telegraphed in return: 'Regret your reply. Cannot make new proposals. Would be grateful for your suggestions.' Molotov did in fact take up the suggestion Tanner had put to Kollontai, for he sent a telegram on 8 February to ask what island Tanner had in mind, and whether it was a firm offer. But before the Finns had the chance to pursue the matter further, the whole situation, both military and political, had undergone a radical change, and with it the basis for the negotiations.[5]

It is now necessary to go back in time in order to trace the evolution of the Anglo-French scheme for a military intervention in the Russo-Finnish war. The French government and public opinion had been the first to react strongly to the Russian attack on Finland; they became increasingly agitated over the situation and possessed by the urge to do something about it. The socialist

[4] *Halsti*, p. 242.
[5] *Tanner*, pp. 146-8: *Jakobson*, pp. 214-5.

97

leader, L. Blum, told an international gathering of socialists that 'in the French parliament and in the realm of
public opinion, there is a powerful desire above all else
to help Finland, whose defeat would be an unprece-
dented catastrophe . . . So we want to do all we can for
Finland, even run the risk of war.' The French government had got hold of the idea that the Finnish war
could be exploited as a means of striking indirectly at
Germany by weakening the Soviet Union. The reasoning
behind this was that Russia was sustaining the German
war economy and frustrating the effects of the Allied
blockade, yet the defeats of the Red Army showed that
Russia was militarily vulnerable. Therefore Germany
could be crippled by attacking Russia, without any need
to fear the consequences. Underlying this rationalization
were two deeper motives: firstly, to divert at any cost
the theatre of action away from the frontiers of France,
into Scandinavia or the Middle East; and secondly to
convert a war against Germany, which to the French
Right at least seemed to have little point after the col-
lapse of Poland, into a war against Bolshevism, which
had much stronger appeal. Already in December French
ruling circles were canvassing two schemes. One was a
plan to use the Polish forces in exile for an expedition
to Petsamo to link up with the Finns, for by using the
Poles as a cover, Britain and France would avoid direct,
formal confrontation with the Soviet Union. The other
plan was to mount air-strikes from the Middle East, with
the connivance of Turkey, at Russia's Caucasian oilfields.
The commander-in-chief, General Gamelin, was initially
sceptical about both ideas, but the government went as
far as discussing the Petsamo plan with Mannerheim,
who rather fancied it, and even provisionally designated
troops and ships to undertake the operation. But nothing
of this sort was possible without the co-operation of
the British, and they were still uninterested in early
December. The British foreign office had even regretted
the proceedings in the League of Nations, and a memorandum had described the expulsion of the Soviet Union

as 'slightly ridiculous'. Although R. A. Butler had assured the Finnish ambassador on 14 December that Britain would give Finland 'the greatest assistance in their power', it was not envisaged in British government circles that this could amount to much.[6]

The beginnings of a serious British involvement in the Russo-Finnish war can be traced to a quite unconnected source. As soon as the war with Germany began the British government, as part of its blockade, became interested in Germany's supplies of iron-ore. Two-fifths of these supplies came from Sweden. In summer they were shipped down the Gulf of Bothnia from Luleå, but in winter, when that route was ice-bound, the ore was sent by rail to Narvik, in Norway, and thence shipped to Germany, using the cover provided by Norwegian territorial waters. Churchill had first suggested blocking this winter route on 19 September; the navy would lay mines in Norwegian territorial waters, forcing the ore ships to go out into the high seas where the navy could stop them.[7] On 16 December Churchill put a specific plan for this to the cabinet: he accepted that it involved a breach of international law, and that Germany would probably retaliate by some kind of counter-action in Scandinavia. But Churchill believed that the Germans, in face of Allied naval superiority, would be at a serious disadvantage, and that any such attack could be met on terms favouring the Allies. This plan, which had nothing to do with Finland, and was perfectly feasible given the resources available, was known subsequently as 'the small plan'.

When the cabinet met on 18 December, to discuss Scandinavia, it had the small plan before it, and also urgings from the French for some kind of Allied response to the Russo-Finnish war and the League of Nations resolution on it. They decided to refer the whole question of Allied military intervention to the chiefs-of-

[6] *Lehmus*, p. 133: *Woodward*, p. 41: M. Gamelin, *Servir*, pp. 193-8. (Hereafter *Gamelin*).
[7] *Woodward*, p. 43.

staff, and to hold off the French proposals for immediate action; so at the meeting of the Allied Supreme War Council on 19 December, the British were quite happy when Gamelin opposed sending direct military aid to Finland, and the Council decided that the Allies should send notes to Norway and Sweden urging them to help Finland on the understanding that if this led to reprisals or military complications they could count on Allied support. The War Council noted that if such assistance did become necessary, it might well offer the Allies an opportunity to cut off the iron ore supply. On 27 December the notes were duly sent to Norway and Sweden, and on 5 January received a firmly negative reply: the two countries would permit the transit of war materials to Finland, and the passage of individual volunteers, but would in no circumstances go beyond this.[8]

In the interim the British chiefs-of-staff had been busy working on the possibilities in Scandinavia and on 2 January they put a new plan before the cabinet, as an alternative to Churchill's idea, which came to be called 'the big plan'. The man behind this was the Chief of the Imperial General Staff, General Ironside, who was obsessed with the need for the Allies to seize the initiative from Germany, partly in order to repair their reputation, which had suffered so badly from the Polish disaster, and partly to throw out of balance the German plans for an offensive in the west. Yet Ironside knew that the Allies did not have the resources for a large-scale military effort. As he contemplated Scandinavia, the idea hardened in his mind that in this theatre a small Allied force could exercise a quite disproportionate effect. He wrote in his diary for 25 December about how 'we ought to do something for Finland' and how there existed in Scandinavia 'the chance of getting a big return for very little expenditure. A chance to take the initiative and throw a little confusion into the German councils.' This was the guiding idea behind the big plan. The plan itself involved the Allies declaring their intention of

8 *Woodward*, pp. 47-8, 56, 57.

sending help to Finland, in conformity with the League of Nations resolution, and demanding that Norway and Sweden give them passage. It was supposed that they would hardly be able to refuse such a request, and the expedition would land at Narvik and proceed down the railway, through the ore fields, to Luleå. There they would set up a base for detaching a force that would operate in Finland. Thus the German ore supplies would be automatically cut off, and when Germany struck back, as she would have to do, the Allies could establish a second front in Scandinavia in conditions favourable to themselves. There are two points to be noticed about this plan. Firstly, Ironside's original conception had been lost from sight at a very early stage, for although he had started by supposing that a force of only 3,000 men would be enough, by 29 December he was writing of the need to be realistic: 'Our effort will be a large one. The expedition itself may be small to begin with, but it will grow to be a major effort.' As so often happens in military planning a conception which began as a small diversion rapidly got out of control. Secondly, Ironside was conscious that giving assistance to Finland was only a pretext: he did not say so in the official papers, but in private conversation he admitted that 'any brigade that reached Finland would remain near the railway and the frontier so as to avoid either getting too close to the Russians, or being cut off by the Germans.'[9]

The cabinet found the concept of the big plan too much for it, particularly since, at that point Chamberlain probably did not like the idea of a Scandinavian adventure in any form, and Halifax certainly did not. The result, in Ironside's words, was that the cabinet 'shied off the bigger issue and took the smaller one of stopping the ore going to Germany' – in other words they preferred the small plan. In consequence, fresh notes were despatched to Norway and Sweden on 6 January, which were intended to prepare the way for

[9] *Woodward*, p. 59: R. Macleod & D. Kelly eds., *The Ironside Diaries*, pp. 185, 188, 191, (Hereafter *Ironside*).

violating neutrality by mining Norwegian territorial waters: it was alleged that their neutrality was conferring unequal advantages on Germany. On 12 January this brought firm replies to the effect that the two countries rejected the Allied contention and would resist infringement of their neutrality, wherever these might come from.[10]

By the time that these replies had come in, the British cabinet was veering round to a different line of policy. Ironside had protested at the decision of 2 January, and submitted a memorandum which argued that to adopt the small plan would only prejudice the much greater advantages inherent in the big plan. Furthermore, French pressures for direct Allied assistance to Finland were building up, and reports had come from Mannerheim's headquarters that if Finnish resistance was to be maintained into the summer, he would need 30,000 fresh troops by May, which could be fitted in with the big plan. So on 11 January, the cabinet revoked the decision of 2 January, cancelled the small plan and authorized the chiefs-of-staff to work out a detailed specification for the big plan. From this point on, the idea of landing some sort of Allied expeditionary force in Scandinavia acquired an unstoppable momentum. Gamelin, who had been unenthusiastic about diversionary operations, sent a memorandum to the French government on 16 January which approved the idea of an expedition to Petsamo. Chamberlain became converted to the concept and henceforth supported it with enthusiasm; he told Ironside that if the Allies gained control of the ore fields, it 'would definitely tip the war over in our favour.' On 27 January, Ironside sent a memorandum to the cabinet on the detailed plans drawn up by the chiefs-of-staff, and stressed that 'intervention in Scandinavia is our first and best chance of wresting the initiative . . . and in fact of shortening the war . . . I feel that now is the moment, however ill-prepared we are in trained troops.' The cabinet approved the plans on 29 January. Two days

[10] *Ironside*, p. 191.

later the chiefs-of-staff met their French opposite numbers and found them still preferring the Petsamo plan,
but when the Supreme War Council met on 5 February,
the British delegation were pleasantly surprised by
Daladier, who readily agreed to drop the French plan
in favour of the British. Even the fact that this involved
diverting British reinforcements that would otherwise
have gone to France did not deter the French, provided
there was to be some definite action in Scandinavia, they
were satisfied.[11]

The plan agreed on by the Allies on 5 February was
that Finland should appeal to them to send assistance
and the Allies would then ask Norway and Sweden to
permit the passage of an expeditionary force. The force
would be technically made up of 'volunteers', and would
operate under Finnish command in northern Finland,
but as a necessary pre-condition, its line of supply would
have to be secured by establishing troops at Narvik and
taking control of the railway from there to the Finnish
frontier. In this way the Swedish ore fields would be
occupied and Germany's supply stopped, but in consequence the southern flank of the operation would have to
be covered by a simultaneous landing of troops at Trondheim, Bergen and Namsos to meet the German riposte
into Norway and Sweden which it was assumed must
follow. The plan required sending two brigades to Narvik and five battalions to the south Norwegian ports,
and then despatching a brigade group on into Finland.
When the Germans struck back a further two divisions
at least would be needed to help Norway and Sweden to
resist. In all it would involve shipping some 100,000
British troops, 50,000 French and giving them the necessary naval and air support. The date for the first landings
was set as 20 March, and the supply convoys would have
to sail on 12 March, which became the key date for the
launching of the expedition.[12]

[11] *Gamelin*, pp. 199-202: *Ironside*, pp. 209, 212: *Woodward*, p. 76:
J. R. M. Butler, *Grand Strategy*, II, p. 107.
[12] *Gamelin*, p. 201: *Ironside*, pp. 215-6: *Woodward*, pp. 79-80.

The formal reasoning of the Supreme War Council was summarized by Ironside as: 'i. That it would be a defeat for us to allow the Finns to be crushed. ii. That we must do something as quickly as possible. iii. That we must demand permission to enter Norway and Sweden. iv. That if we couldn't gain the acquiescence of the Norwegians and Swedes, we must try the Petsamo project.' On this basis the proposal looks like a Quixotic folly for the Allies at a time when they were engaged in a mortal conflict with Germany that required all their strength. But in fact the Council was being much more realistic than Ironside's summary might suggest: the Allied planners had no illusions about the real purpose behind their scheme. Chamberlain spoke quite frankly when he put the British plan to the Council. It was 'ostensibly and nominally designed for the assistance of Finland' but in fact designed to seize the iron-ore and provoke a German reaction – it would, he said, 'kill two birds with one stone.' Ironside wrote in his diary: 'We must see we are politically strong and that we remain quite cynical about everything, except stopping the iron-ore. We could not create a better diversion than this.' Gamelin expressed his support for the plan, including the withholding of troops from France, 'because it was evident that the bulk of the expeditionary force would be called to operate against the Germans.'[13]

Thus the plan was not such a folly as it appears at first sight. Only a token brigade of 'volunteers' would go and fight in Finland; there would be no need for Britain and France to declare war on the Soviet Union. The Allied plan was a device for pursuing their war with Germany in Scandinavia, using the need to help Finland as the legal excuse for violating the neutrality of Norway and Sweden, and provoking the necessary German retaliation. The Allies were right to count on this, for Hitler had ordered planning for a counter-stroke to an Allied intervention in Scandinavia as far back as 14

[13] *Ironside*, p. 215: *Gamelin*, p. 202.

December, and by February the German preparations were well advanced. The major weakness of the Allied plan was that it hinged entirely on Norway and Sweden giving their consent, for there was no thought at this stage of proceeding against their resistance. But as General Pownall, chief-of-staff to the British forces in France, wrote when he came to hear of it: 'I cannot for the life of me see why they should agree, for what do they get out of it except the certainty that Germany will declare war on them and part of their countries at least will be used as a battle-ground.' All that the promoters of the plan could say in reply was that once Finland had formally appealed for help to the Allies, moral pressure and public opinion in Norway and Sweden would compel their governments to grant passage whatever they might say to the contrary. The whole Allied project was a gamble on this intuition proving correct, and that is the measure of its basic unsound ness.[14]

The other major weakness of the project was that it was by no means certain that Finland would agree to play her allotted role in it, for with very few exceptions the Finnish leaders seem to have sensed that the Allied offer of assistance was basically fraudulent, and in so far as it was genuine, would be quite inadequate. Initially, contact between Finland and the Allies was in the hands of the military leadership. Mannerheim handled them himself, working through the Allied representatives at his headquarters, and through the Finnish representatives in Paris, the ambassador H. Holma, and the military attaché Colonel Paasonen. The government, and in particular Tanner, were not very closely informed, and Tanner was none too pleased when he did hear of what was developing, for he feared that any Allied offer would be seized on by those in the government who opposed his desire for a speedily-negotiated peace. On the other hand, Ryti and Paasikivi welcomed the news of the Allied

14 B. Bond ed., *Chief of Staff: the diaries of Lieutenant General Sir Henry Pownall*, I, p. 281. (Hereafter *Pownall*).

proposals since they believed that it could be used as a bargaining counter. Finland could either force the Soviet Union to moderate her demands, by threatening to appeal to the Allies, or use the same threat to blackmail Sweden into giving more active assistance – nobody of consequence in the Finnish leadership wanted the actual assistance, they just wanted to exploit the threat of it for their own ends. Ironside may have prided himself on his cynical realism over this project, but he met his match in Mannerheim, Ryti, Tanner and Paasikivi. Even so, the Allied decision of 5 February necessarily became a major factor in Finnish calculations as soon as it was known.

Between 8 and 12 February there were intensive consultations in Finland to work out how to handle the situation. On 8 February, Tanner, Ryti, Paasikivi and General Walden, who was Mannerheim's representative, met and agreed that more concessions would have to be offered in order to get negotiations started, and that for this purpose it would be necessary to reveal the secret contacts with Moscow to a wider circle. They began with president Kallio, who was initially displeased with the development, and then on 10 February summoned a formal meeting of the Defence Council at Mannerheim's headquarters. The Defence Council agreed to a scheme of priorities set out by Tanner. First they would try direct negotiations with Russia. Failing that they would try to persuade Sweden to join the war, and only as a last resort might they appeal to the Allies. It was also agreed that Russia could be offered more territory on the Karelian isthmus and the island of Jussarö as a base in the Gulf of Finland, but Russia would be expected to give compensation. Armed with these agreements, Tanner and Ryti then tackled their ministerial colleagues at a meeting of the foreign affairs committee of the government on 12 February. Kallio reluctantly agreed to back the new concessions, but the six ministers were split evenly, Ryti, Tanner and Paasikivi in favour, Hannula, Niukkanen and Söderhjelm against. This group was rigidly opposed to making any fresh concessions to the Soviet Union and alleged that in any case parliament would never ratify an agreement on such terms. They therefore preferred to appeal to the Allies rather than make fresh concessions to the Russians. In these circumstances all that could be agreed was that Tanner should go to Stockholm and ask the Swedish government for its active intervention in the war. However, the ruling junta, meeting afterwards, decided that Tanner could inform the Russians of the concessions approved by the Defence Council, and Tanner set off for Stockholm the same day. Before the process of negotiation could proceed any further, however, the situation was transformed when the Russians forced an irreparable breach in the Mannerheim line.[15]

When it had become clear in December that the Russian offensive on the isthmus had failed, Stalin was understandably angry. He told Meretskov that not only was the military fiasco damaging Russian policy in general, but it threatened to undermine the military credibility of the Red Army. The first step was to reorganize the Russian command. On 26 December, the isthmus front was divided and the right wing entrusted to a new XIII Army under General V. D. Grendal, while Meretskov retained command of VII Army on the left. Then, on 7 January, the whole Finnish theatre of war was made into a new north-western front under the command of General S. K. Timoshenko; thus the pretence that the Finnish campaign was solely the affair of the Leningrad military district was dropped. Stalin demanded a new offensive based on thorough preparation; the first step being to discover exactly what the Russians were up against by intensive air reconnaissance and patrol activity on land. Meretskov describes special patrols sent through the Finnish positions to get samples of the concrete from the Finnish bunkers for analysis, and says that it took most of January to build up a complete picture of the enemy defences. While this was being

15 *Tanner*, pp. 150-6: *Paasikivi*, p. 147: *Jakobson*, pp. 223-5.

done, the army was renovated, partly by moving in fresh, first-class units, partly by providing new equipment like the KV tank, flame-throwing tanks and armoured sledges for the infantry, which would play an important role in the new offensive. Above all, the Russians called in masses of fresh artillery. This revitalized army was then put through a course of intensive re-training: new operational orders had been issued on 28 December which involved a complete change of tactics. There was now to be a methodical advance, step by step, with all arms in close co-operation. Mass infantry assaults were to be discontinued; instead positions would be properly softened up before the infantry were sent in. The quality of clothing and supplies was to be improved, and in every department careful and meticulous advance planning was to be the rule. To facilitate this, models of the Finnish positions were built, and throughout January realistic battle training was conducted over them. During this period the Russian main force was not in close contact with the enemy, but the Finns could hear the noise of the training schemes from their own lines. The final plan was approved at a conference between Stalin, Molotov and Zhdanov on the political side, and Voroshilov, Timoshenko, Meretskov, Grendal and the famous artillery expert, General Voronov. The plan hinged on Voronov's artillery preparation, which involved guns of up to 280-mm firing over open sights and without pause for a prolonged period of time. Stalin insisted that the Finnish resistance must be broken before the spring thaw, and VII Army must reach the line from Viipuri to Antrea, while XIII Army advanced to the line from Antrea to Käkisalmi; they would then be in a position, if the Finns continued the war, to advance into the heart of Finland.[16]

The Finnish command had had no comparable opportunity to make counter preparations. 5 Division, which had taken the brunt of the December fighting had been replaced on the vital Summa sector by 3 Division, and

[16] *Erikson*, pp. 548-50: *Meretskov*, pp. 185-7.

had moved into reserve. Otherwise the same units were in the same positions; 4 Division held the coastal sector, 1 and 2 Divisions the line between Summa and the Vuoksi. III Army Corps held the line of the Vuoksi to Lake Ladoga with its original two divisions. The Finns had also built up a strategic reserve of two new divisions, 21 and 23 Divisions, made up of reservists and incompletely equipped. These were really second-line troops since, apart from their deficiencies of equipment, they also had very low quotas of professional officers. The reserve force had been set to work preparing two further lines of defence. The first of these was known as the 'intermediate position' and consisted of field works with wire and tank obstacles – it was conceived of as a delaying position only. The other, the 'rear position', was anchored on the city of Viipuri and ran through Tali and Kuparsaari to the Vuoksi. This was a line of considerable potential strength; the terrain was rocky and difficult for an attacker, and some of it could be flooded. It was planned to build concrete bunkers, for which civilian labour had been brought in, but the work was still far from complete in February.

The front remained fairly quiet until 15 January when Russian artillery preparation began against 3 Division. On the very first day the bunkers sustained hits from heavy shells, so that on the day following the division had to call for additional engineers to repair them. This started a pattern of activity which lasted for two weeks; each day the bunkers were damaged and each night they had to be repaired. The Russians could fire undisturbed, over open sights, and had the assistance of continuous aerial observation. The Russian planes harassed anything that moved by daylight, so that, in spite of the vicious cold it was dangerous for the Finns to heat tents and dugouts, as the smoke rising in the still clear air would betray their position. But this was only the preliminary softening up; the real battle began on 1 February with a barrage of massive proportions against the Summa positions. The Russians were using about 400 guns at a density of fifty guns to the kilometre. VII Army had twelve rifle divisions, of which nine were in line for the initial assault, backed by five tank brigades and a number of specialist units, including assault teams for tackling the bunkers. XIII Army had nine rifle divisions, of which five were in line for the initial attack, supported by a single tank brigade.

The Russian attacks were led by tanks and small specialist units which concentrated on the bunkers and on clearing tank obstacles and minefields: the tanks could often make the bunkers unusable by parking in front of the gun slits and firing straight into them. This exploited the two main weaknesses of these bunkers: they could not usually support one another by cross fire and they had no anti-tank guns. The Finnish defenders often had to abandon the bunkers during daylight, and re-occupy and repair them at night. One serious consequence of this was the loss of the use of the bunkers as warm, secure billets – the men lay out in the bitter cold all day and worked all night restoring the position. Gradually the physical stamina of the men was worn down, yet there were no reliefs – even the units not actually in the front line had to spend their nights moving supplies and helping with repairs. The initial pressure lasted for three days, followed by a pause during which the Finns could have taken 3 Division out of the line and relieved it with 5 Division, as the local commander was urging, but this was not done. On 5 February the attack started up again for another three days, and by 8 February General Öhqvist noted that 3 Division 'are deadly tired and absolutely must be relieved, but headquarters still refuses to release 5 Division in their place.' Therefore Öhqvist suggested to 3 Division commander that at least he could relieve his worst pressed battalion at Summa, and this was done on 9 February, when the Russian pressure again slackened. Öhqvist's other main worry was the shortage of shells: on 8 February he had to order his artillery to restrict its firing to what was 'absolutely necessary for keeping possession of our positions.' Up to this point, the Russians had made no permanent breach in the Finnish line, and where they had secured a lodgement they had been driven out again – but on Sunday, 11 February, the situation changed.[17]

The break occurred on a stretch of the front between Lake Summa and a frozen swamp, where a main road went through towards Viipuri. It had five concrete bunkers, but only two were of much use, and the sector was held by an under-strength battalion of only 400 men which had only taken over its positions on 9 February, and was not properly settled in. The break was achieved by the Russian 123 Division, supported by a strong force of tanks. On the main axis of advance the Finns did not have a single anti-tank gun in working order. The tanks blocked the main bunker and at about midday its defenders abandoned it, some in panic. The other principal bunker fought on all day until the Russians destroyed it and its garrison. By the evening of 11 February, the Russians had broken through to the rear of the position and dug themselves in. Öhqvist now had no choice but to use the only reserve, 5 Division, to try and restore his front, but though this was ordered at once the move could not be executed until after dark on 12 February, and the counter-attack failed. The Finns fought on through 13 February, clinging to the rear of their position, but in the afternoon the line broke and Russian tanks moved out into the open country beyond, where they overran a Finnish battery. Öhqvist recognized that the position was lost and proposed to evacuate the Mannerheim line and pull back his troops to the intermediate position. Mannerheim gave permission on 15 February, and the general retreat to the intermediate position was completed successfully on 17 February.

Thus the Red Army finally broke the Mannerheim line after two weeks of intensive fighting, though only at one point – the rest of the line had been held intact. But one breach was enough and it was the military turn-

[17] *Halsti*, pp. 262, 263.

ing point of the war. Many and complex reasons can be advanced for the Russian success: their own careful preparations which skilfully exploited the original Finnish mistakes in the siting and equipment of the bunkers; the fact that the main Finnish reserve, 5 Division, was held too far behind the front and released too late by a reluctant headquarters. But the essential factor was undoubtedly attrition – the Finns did not have enough shells, did not have enough anti-tank guns, above all did not have enough men. Their front-line units were all under strength because their replacements had been taken to form new units, and all they were offered to make up losses were recruits so raw that some commanders were reluctant to accept them. These under-strength units had been under growing strain since 15 January, worn down by incessant gunfire, aerial harassment, savage cold and, above all, lack of rest in reasonably warm, secure billets. Simply because there was no possibility of relief, the front-line troops suffered an insidious, creeping loss of physical and mental stamina. In these conditions, if the Russians could keep up their pressure for long enough, the defence was bound to crack in the end – even the best troops in the world must be able to sleep, and this was virtually denied to these Finnish soldiers.

The occupation of the intermediate position was complicated by two factors. Firstly, Mannerheim had ordered the holding of the island of Koivisto, with its heavy batteries, to harass the Russian flank and this required the diversion of some forces and lengthened the front. Secondly, on 15 February, Russian bombers blocked the Sortavala-Viipuri railway along which the Finnish 23 Division was moving up to the front, and significantly delayed its arrival. This meant that when the Russians began probing the intermediate position on 17 February it was not fully manned and organized, and it was ominous that by 19 February Russian tanks had made firm inroads into the defences at their weakest point – a stretch of open, sandy terrain in the Näykkijärvi-

Mustalampi sector. It was the more ominous because they had done this without artillery support, for the Russian guns had not then come up in force, and it was no longer easy to drive the tanks out again. They now stayed fairly close to their infantry, could not be attacked in daylight in open country, and had learned to set guards at night to keep off Finnish attackers. The problems of the Finnish anti-tank defences on this sector are illustrated by the fate of a detachment which went into action on 15 February with two anti-tank guns. These were loaded on a lorry, while the crews had come straight from training school, without seeing their weapons in advance. The following day the survivors returned to the rear, having lost both the guns and half their comrades. When they had got to the line under cover of darkness and unloaded the guns, they discovered that these were of a foreign type which the men did not know how to use. Before they could find out the Russian tanks had overrun them and the survivors fled. On the coast, the Russian advance quickly threatened to cut off Koivisto, which had to be evacuated on 22 February and the batteries blown up. Although the rest of the intermediate position was substantially intact, the position was worrying, for there were signs everywhere that the Finnish troops were losing some of their effectiveness through exhaustion.

For this reason Öhqvist suggested to his superiors that preparations be made to withdraw to the rear position because 'there are unending crises and the troops are worn out, and there is a great danger looming that the intermediate position will not hold for long.' Mannerheim responded that 'he was astonished that we should even think of the possibility that the intermediate position should be given up', and ordered that it must be held to the last. Following this, Mannerheim reshuffled his commanders. Österman was relieved of the command of the Karelian Army, Heinrichs left III Army Corps to replace him, and Talvela came from the Tolvajärvi sector to take command of the defence of Vuoksi.

But this could not alter the fact that Russian pressure was building up and the line looked increasingly vulnerable. Öhqvist was joined by his new superior, Heinrichs, in pressing for permission to prepare a retreat and on 23 February Mannerheim agreed, accepting that once the Russians launched a proper assault with artillery support the intermediate position could not hold for long. Öhqvist was more pessimistic – he reckoned that the tanks alone could probably force a breach. Mannerheim's attitude was dictated more by political than military considerations; he knew that peace negotiations were in progress and believed, in his old-fashioned way, that by holding on to as much territory as possible, Finland's negotiating position would be strengthened. He wrote: 'The fact that peace-feelers were still being developed gave me cause to stress once again to the new commander of the isthmus army how necessary it was that the intermediate position be held, however difficult the situation might seem.' But Öhqvist had assessed the possibilities correctly. On 25 February the line broke in the Näykkijärvi sector: the Finnish 13 Infantry Regiment, which had been in action continuously since 11 February, and had companies of forty to fifty men, gave way. On the morning of 26 February the Finns tried to close the gap with a counter-attack, using their only fifteen serviceable tanks. Using the tanks proved to be a mistake: in moving up they caused panic in the Finnish rear, since it was assumed that any tanks must be Russian, and in the subsequent action over half were lost and nothing was achieved. They were only Vickers light tanks, with an improvised 37-mm gun, and were no match for the 28-ton tanks used by the Russians. The counter-attack failed to shift the Russians and that same evening Mannerheim ordered a retreat to the rear position. By defending the intermediate position the Finns had won about twelve days, during which time peace negotiations had developed and the rear position was being further prepared. But because of the condition of the intermediate position, and the declining

fighting efficiency of the troops the Finnish casualty rate
had risen alarmingly. It is always the case in war that when
raw troops are thrown straight into action, without any
time to adapt to the realities of warfare, they are sus-
ceptible to unusually high losses, and the same is true of
experienced troops when they become too tired to care. It
was fortunate for the Finns that the Russians stuck to
their revised tactics: they did not press hard on the
retreating enemy, but were content to follow up slowly.[18]

The rear position was potentially a strong one and a
considerable civilian work force had been preparing it.
This was necessary because the rocky, broken terrain,
though very difficult for tanks, was also virtually impossible to dig in, and carried an additional hazard from
rock splinters created by bursting shells. At the end of
February, the tank obstacles, wire and dugouts were
more or less complete, but in some parts the actual
trenches and gun pits were unfinished. The most open
section of the line, the Tali sector, had been flooded,
but in the prevailing conditions the flood waters were
freezing hard. More serious was the position on the right
flank, where the line rested on the Gulf of Finland and
depended on a string of fortified islands in the approaches
to Viipuri. Here the sea-ice was strong enough to carry
tanks, and the Finnish efforts to saw or blow holes in the
ice were frustrated by the continuing cold. This was the
real weak spot, for the coast and archipelago were held
by coast defence units, unequipped and untrained for
field operations, nor could defences be improvised in the
rocky terrain. The Finnish command tried to cover
this danger when, on 18 February, General Wallenius
was brought from the Salla front with troops relieved by
the Swedish volunteer battalion, and took command of
the Coast Group. But his command was a rag-bag collection of disparate units, and the poor communications in
the sector hampered organization, on top of which, on
3 March, Mannerheim replaced Wallenius by General
K. L. Oesch. Thus the Coast Group entered the battle

18 *Halsti*, pp. 317, 318, 321.

under all the worst handicaps of hasty improvization.

Otherwise the retreat went well. 3 Division, which had been withdrawn after the Summa fighting, and rested and refitted to some extent, was in position round Viipuri and ready to meet the Russian advance. The other units disengaged successfully from the intermediate position and fell back into place on the rear position. Nowhere did the Russians pursue closely, and it was not until 2 March that there was general contact with the enemy along the new line. But there was one exception, and this was on the coast, where the Russians pressed boldly over the ice to capture the island of Teikarsaari, west of Viipuri, on 2 March and then began to push patrols towards the mainland. This was the first stage of the Russian plan to break the rear position, and clear the whole area up to the Viipuri-Käkisalmi line. It involved the hazardous decision to use the reserves of VII Army, which consisted of XVIII Army Corps, in an offensive across the open ice-field towards the coast at Vilajoki. Once the Russians were established ashore they had not far to go before cutting the main Viipuri-Helsinki road, thus threatening the total isolation of Viipuri and turning the whole right flank of the Finnish defences. The main body of VII Army would close on Viipuri from the south, but its principal effort would be on the Tali sector, the weakest and most open part of the Finnish line. On the Russian right XIII Army, which up to this point had had little success, and whose commander had been relieved on 2 March, was to attack Vuosalmi where the rear position joined the Vuoksi. Vuosalmi was another weak spot, the river there was frozen solid, the Finns had few prepared positions and again a rocky terrain made it difficult to improvise defences. Success at Vuosalmi would have made the position of III Army Corps on the lower Vuoksi untenable, and could conceivably have led to its being cut off and destroyed. Indeed the Finnish command took a calculated risk in leaving both III and IV Army Corps in their exposed positions, for if the Russians did break through at Viipuri these units would be cut off from the rest of the Finnish army. Mannerheim, obsessed with the need to hang on to territory as a bargaining counter, was gambling on holding the rear position until either peace was concluded, or the thaw began and halted operations. He was lucky, as it happened, but it was nevertheless a fearful risk.

The city of Viipuri, the second city of Finland, was held by the Finnish 3 and 5 Divisions, and pressure on them began on 3 March. The significant development on this sector was the steady stripping of their reserves to build up the Coast Group: one regiment left on 3 March, and was followed by anti-tank units and artillery; and then on 7 March another regiment went, so that the whole of II Army Corps' reserves were either already engaged on the coastal sector or on their way to it, leaving the two divisions defending Viipuri with only two of their three regiments and these all fully engaged in the front line. On 8 March the consequences began to show when the Russians made the first serious dents in the defences of the city; by 11 March, Öhqvist knew that they could not hold the city much longer. Mannerheim, however, insisted that the defenders must hold out, which they did. On 12 March the Russians had got close to the city centre, but when fighting ceased on the following day the city of Viipuri was mostly in Finnish hands – but only just. Events in Viipuri had demonstrated once more that even the best troops cannot sustain a prolonged defence against a superior enemy when there is no possibility of rest or reinforcement.[19]

One of the worst trials experienced by the defenders of Viipuri, or at least by their commanders (who knew what was happening), was the progress made by the Russians over the ice to the west of the city. On this sector, the Finnish 4 Division and the conglomeration of different units that constituted the Coast Group tried to beat the attackers back. The Russians had the advantage that the sea-ice would carry light tanks, and these compensated for the lack of artillery support and the

[19] *Halsti*, p. 363.

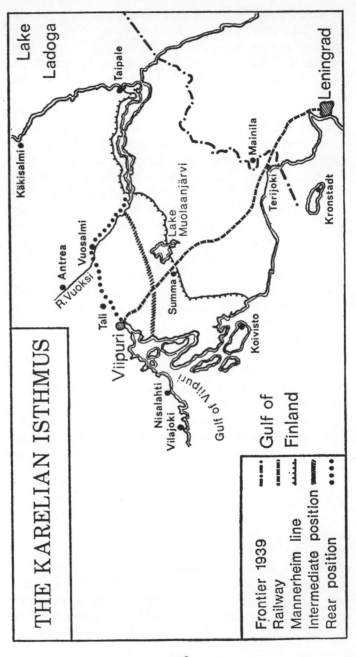

THE KARELIAN ISTHMUS

Lake Ladoga

Taipale

Käkisalmi

Antrea

Vuosalmi

R. Vuoksi

Tali

Viipuri

Nisalahti

Vilajoki

Gulf of Viipuri

Koivisto

Summa

Lake Muolaanjärvi

Mainila

Terijoki

Kronstadt

Leningrad

Gulf of Finland

Frontier 1939
Railway
Mannerheim line
Intermediate position
Rear position

absence of cover on the ice-field. The attackers were not always successful however. The most westerly columns in the Virolahti-Kotka sector never got ashore, but were repelled on the ice by the Finnish coastal batteries and turned back. It is probable that these moves were only meant to tie down the Finnish forces, and this they succeeded in doing while the real threat developed elsewhere. There was one thrust close to Viipuri, which came over the islands in the Gulf of Viipuri against 4 Division, and this was the most dangerous because of the immediate threat of isolating the defenders of the city. Further to the west the Russians came ashore in the Vilajoki-Nisalahti sector of the mainland and began to establish a formidable bridgehead. The Russian tactics were skilful: the light tanks were too small to climb the rocky shores from the ice, or to make their way through deep snow where it was possible to get ashore. Furthermore, they were vulnerable to any kind of artillery fire – one Finnish battalion claimed to have knocked out four of them with a pre-1918 gun left behind as obsolete by the Tsarist garrison. But the tanks could shelter infantry crossing the ice, provide off-shore covering-fire when the infantry tried to land tow men and supplies in armoured sledges, and, where there were islands, could blockade the Finnish defenders by cruising round them on the ice and cutting their communications.

The Finnish command sent in all the reserves it could scrape up, but these were not sufficient to hold the Russians. By 7 March the main Viipuri-Helsinki road was under fire, which forced the Coast Group to reorganize in two commands on either side of the bridgehead and created communication and supply difficulties. When the fighting ended the Finnish forces were preparing a counter-attack designed to eliminate the growing threat. They had brought up the Cavalry Brigade from IV Army Corps front and planned to eliminate the Vilajoki-Nisalahti bridgehead by a concerted attack on its two flanks. This operation might have succeeded, for the Russian troops in the bridgehead had no heavy equipment with them. On the other hand, the Finns were short of shells – on 4 March II Army Corps had had only 600 artillery shells in its stores. The Russian venture over the sea-ice was certainly a gamble, for any sudden change of weather that caused the ice to break up would have left them stranded with no communications, while the Finnish counter-attack could have destroyed them, or forced a precarious retreat. Yet even if the worst had happened, the Russian gamble would have paid off, for by drawing in all the available Finnish reserves to this sector, the Russians had virtually guaranteed a break-through elsewhere. They were on the verge of achieving this at two points when the fighting stopped.

The first of these was at the Tali sector where the Finnish 23 Division, a unit made up of reservists with very few regular officers, proved unequal to its task. The Finns were helped by flooding, which restricted the Russian freedom of movement, though in many places the flood waters froze hard enough for infantry to cross. But they were weakened by the fact that their reserve regiment was taken away to defend the coast, by the loss of most of their anti-tank guns in earlier fighting and by their shortage of artillery ammunition. As soon as the Russians came up in force, on 5 March, 23 Division began to give ground, and the Finnish command became alarmed at the increasing signs of sagging morale and a weakening will to fight. On 8 March one whole battalion fled in panic, though it was not under direct attack, and the Russians showed themselves bold and enterprising. When the Russians halted, on 12 March, after advancing slowly but continuously for a week, it was not the resistance of 23 Division that stopped them, but growing supply difficulties and the need to regroup and bring up their artillery across the flood zone for the next stage of the attack. At the end of the war, the Russians were poised for a breakthrough at Tali and it would have needed fresh forces to stop them.

The second threatened breakthrough developed at

Vuosalmi, where the rear position joined the River Vuoksi. The Finnish 23 Infantry Regiment had had to improvise a defensive bridgehead on the west bank because of the lie of the land, and because there were no prepared defences. The ground was too rocky to dig proper field-works, and the Finns had to make do with holes in the snow. The river was frozen, and though some gaps were made and kept open in the ice, it was nevertheless possible for infantry to cross. Because of the lack of proper positions and because here, as elsewhere, the Finnish artillery was too short of ammunition to give adequate covering fire, the infantry defending this sector suffered unusually high casualties. The Russians arrived before the position on 29 February, and launched their first serious attack on 2 March with a whole division, a second one coming up in support. The Finnish III Army Corps had as its reserve 21 Division, another unit created out of reservists, and lacking one of its regiments; and this was ordered to take over the defence of Vuosalmi. But before the main body could arrive, the Russians had forced a crossing of the river, and they beat off the Finnish counter-attacks, mainly because of the weakness of the Finnish artillery – in contrast the Russians had ample guns firing over open sights. So even the arrival of the main body of 21 Division on 8 March could not stop the Russian advance, and though its troops fought well, by 13 March the Russians had established a solid bridgehead over the Vuoksi, while the Finnish defenders were showing signs of exhaustion.

The general military situation on 13 March can be summarized as follows. The Russian offensive on the isthmus showed no signs of slackening and the Russians were probably in a position to achieve their objective – the line Viipuri-Antrea-Käkisalmi – before the spring thaw stopped operations. In addition they were preparing to resume the offensive north of Lake Ladoga. The Finns had committed their whole available force to battle, and could only reinforce the isthmus front by taking men from the eastern front, giving up territory as necessary – even then these troops would need several days to move south, and were in any case battle-weary. The opinion of Öhqvist and Oesch, who commanded the Coast Group, was that by 13 March a general retreat was necessary if the Finnish field army was to be preserved intact. This would mean evacuating the III Army Corps from the Vuoksi and the IV Army Corps from north of Ladoga, and trying to hold the line Virolahti-Vuoksenniska-Hiitola-Ladoga-Jänisjärvi until the thaw. This was militarily feasible provided that the Russians did not break the southern anchor of the line from their Vilajoki bridgehead, and did not make a vigorous pursuit, something they had not so far done. But after that, unless big reinforcements of men and material were secured, the total defeat of the Finnish army in a summer campaign was certain. There were two ominous sets of statistics which made this conclusion unavoidable. Despite increased domestic production and imports, the stocks of artillery ammunition were lower in March than at the outbreak of hostilities, and there was no prospect of raising them quickly to adequate levels. This was crucial because only through abundant artillery support could the Finns compensate for their lack of numbers and their inferior equipment. The other sinister figures were those for available manpower. The original front-line strength of the Finnish infantry had been about 150,000 men, but by March, casualties and general attrition had removed some 80,000 men from the ranks. The remaining reservists, added to the 1940 class of conscripts, would yield about 170,000 recruits, but even if their training was cut down to a bare minimum and they were thrown straight into battle, it would have been May or June before most of these reinforcements could be used. Until then, the original field army would have to fight on at about half its nominal strength. In short, by 13 March the war was lost unless significant new forces were added to the Finnish side, something equivalent to six fresh divisions, together with adequate artillery, anti-tank weapons and basic air support. The

Finnish decision to make peace in March 1940 was based ultimately on these harsh military realities.

It will be recalled that on 12 February the Finnish government had decided that Tanner should go to Stockholm in order to clarify the Swedish position, and that Tanner and the inner group of ministers had resolved privately that they would offer the Russians an island, Jussarö, in place of Hanko. Tanner's mission was doomed before he set out, for on that same day the Soviet government, presumably confident that military success was now within its grasp, had raised its terms. The Swedish government was informed that the Russians would require Hanko and the cession of the whole Karelian isthmus, thus making Jussarö's offer irrelevant. Nor was there any prospect of a change in the policy of Sweden. The position had been debated in the Swedish parliament on 17 January, but the minority of conservative critics who wanted something more to be done for Finland had not advanced any concrete suggestions. The former foreign minister, Sandler, had mentioned his old plan for joining Finland in the defence of the Åland islands, and had warned that if Sweden did not help Finland then the Allies would intervene and turn Scandinavia into a battlefield, but he made no further practical proposals.[20]

Thus, when Tanner met the Swedish prime minister, foreign minister and defence minister on 13 February, the Swedes could claim that they spoke for all informed political opinion in the country when they refused the request that Sweden should raise the level of her assistance. Specifically, they rejected the idea, already canvassed by Ryti during a visit to Stockholm in January, that complete units of the Swedish army might serve in Finland as 'volunteers', and added that in no circumstances could they permit the passage of Allied troops across Swedish territory. The Swedish ministers claimed that their position was dictated by the attitude of Germany, which had stated that it would intervene against

[20] *Paasikivi*, pp. 140-1; *Jakobson*, pp. 226-8.

Sweden if any additional help were given to Finland. This story was a complete fabrication, as both Tanner and the Swedes well knew. There was no threat of German interference, provided Sweden acted by herself, and this policy had been confirmed in a German foreign office memorandum as recently as 10 February. Only if Allied forces established themselves in Sweden would the Germans intervene. It is clear that the Swedish leaders clung to this falsehood in order to provide some moral covering for the brutal realism of their calculations: they knew that Finland could make peace with Russia on terms that would preserve her independence, and would leave Finland as a buffer state between Sweden and the Soviet Union. On the other hand, if the war continued, it was almost certain that the Allies would intervene and drag Sweden into a general European war. So the Swedish leaders had every incentive to discourage Finland from continuing to fight and to urge the Finnish government to accept the Russian terms.[21]

Tanner's visit to Stockholm, therefore, brought Finland no encouragement; on the contrary it resulted in a nasty and upsetting incident between the two countries. On 16 February a Stockholm newspaper published a story that Tanner had come to ask for Swedish military intervention, which had been refused. When Hansson was asked to comment on this he said that the government's policy, as stated in parliament on 17 January, was unchanged and that Tanner's request 'that Swedish military units be moved into Finland' had been turned down. In Finland this statement was regarded as a betrayal which could only undermine Finland's bargaining position against Russia, and it caused deep resentment. Even in Sweden the general public became disturbed, to such an extent that on 19 February the king of Sweden issued a personal statement which confirmed, though in more tactful language and with expressions of regret, what Hansson had said. The king summarized

[21] *Tanner*, pp. 157-60: *Jakobson*, pp. 228-9.

Sweden's attitude when he concluded: 'I am convinced that if Sweden intervened in the Finnish war, we would be in the greatest danger of being drawn not only into the war with Russia, but also into the war between the great powers.' As Tanner commented, 'the royal statement definitely ended hope of aid from Sweden.'[22]

The German government was still interested at this stage in getting an early end to the war, which threatened Hitler's chosen policy of preserving the neutrality of Scandinavia. Despite some lobbying from Admiral Raeder in December in favour of securing Norwegian bases for the German submarine campaign, Hitler had remained unmoved. It was the Allied notes to Norway and Sweden on 6 January that alerted Hitler to the danger of an Allied intervention in Scandinavia, and led him on 10 January to order a study of possible German counter action. This in turn led to the idea of Germany striking first and forestalling the Allies, and on 23 January the actual planning for such an operation, code named 'Weserübung', was authorized. But it was still the hope of the German leadership that the Finnish war could be wound up and a Scandinavian complication avoided. This was demonstrated on 13 February when von Ribbentrop instructed Blücher to suggest to the Finnish government that Germany might facilitate a meeting in Berlin between a Finnish and a Russian representative to discuss peace terms. When Blücher put the idea to Tanner on 17 February he did not know that contacts had already been established through Stockholm, so that his proposal was not attractive to Finland. Tanner, however, felt it was worthwhile to probe into what lay behind the German move, and expressed interest. Before the matter could be carried further, the situation in Berlin was changed because of Hitler's furious reaction to the *Altmark* incident on 17 February. He determined to go ahead with 'Weserübung' and seize Denmark and Norway before the Allies could act; the formal directive for this was issued on 1 March and the timetable was laid

[22] *Tanner*, pp. 160-3: *Mannerheim*, p. 252.

down on 3 March. The change in German policy meant that it no longer mattered to Hitler if the Finnish war continued but it became more important than ever to preserve the good-will of the Soviet Union by a scrupulous respect for the free hand over Finland, which was enshrined in the August agreements. Therefore Blücher was told to withdraw his suggestion, which he did in an interview with Tanner on 20 February, pretending that it had been a private initiative of his own, about whose prospects of success he could give no assurance. Tanner affected to be deeply offended and virtually showed the ambassador the door, so that Blücher reported back to Berlin that he was sure Finland had committed herself to the Allies. With this episode, Germany's involvement in the war between Russia and Finland virtually ended. Unofficial messages continued to reach the Finns from various German sources, and all urged Finland to accept any terms that Russia might offer, but officially Germany washed her hands of the whole business.[23]

The negative attitude of the Swedish government was still not sufficient to persuade most Finnish political leaders of the need to accept the Russian peace terms. Paasikivi understood, for he wrote in his diary on 17 February, 'for a long time we have been living in the grip of delusions', and he listed seven of them, including the belief that Sweden would intervene militarily ('that delusion has collapsed') and more recently the belief that the Allies would rescue Finland. But there were not many as clear-sighted as Paasikivi. Tanner was one of the exceptions, and he was now bent on winning his colleagues round to making peace. On 21 February Tanner revealed to the foreign affairs committee of parliament, in cautious terms, that a negotiated peace with Russia was now possible but that the concessions demanded would go beyond those put forward in October. The committee's response enabled Tanner to ask the Swedish government to tell Moscow that it was ready to continue its mediation on the basis of the latest terms. On 23 February

23 *DGFP*, pp. 774, 778, 785: *Tanner*, pp. 165-7.

the foreign affairs committee of the government met to consider the position. It had before it a report on the Allied offer of assistance, and was given to understand that this was equivalent to some three and a half divisions, but that it could only be implemented with the consent of Norway and Sweden. The committee also had a warning from Finnish headquarters that the troops were getting dangerously exhausted. But the ministers could not make up their minds to open direct negotiations on the Russian conditions; all they could agree upon was to wait until Sweden had once more been asked to send troops, or to let the Allies do so, and until Britain and France provided more particulars of when their assistance would arrive.[24]

The next step was a formal meeting of the government, with the president in the chair, on 25 February. By this time the situation had clarified a little further: the Soviet government, in reply to the message from the Swedish government, had communicated its terms more precisely. They were the surrender of Hanko as a base for thirty years, the cession of the whole of the Karelian isthmus up to the line of Peter the Great's frontier of 1721, which meant the loss of the towns of Viipuri and Sortavala, and the conclusion of a mutual assistance pact between Russia, Finland and Estonia for the defence of the Gulf of Finland. The Swedish government had re-affirmed its position on both military intervention and the transit of Allied troops, and the Allied representatives in Finland had quoted a figure for their expeditionary force of 20-24,000 men, to be in Finland by 15 April. This last information was a bait to lure the Finns into accepting Allied aid, for when the British foreign office heard that its ambassador had been using these figures, it instructed him on 27 February to tell the Finns the truth – the proposed expedition would total 12-13,000 men and it would arrive at the end of April. The good effect which the figures should have had on the Finns was undermined by the vagueness

24 *Paasikivi*, pp. 148, 150-2: *Tanner*, pp. 170-2.

of the Allied representatives when asked how the expedition would get to Finland; they could only assert that if Finland would issue a call for help, then Norway and Sweden must yield to moral persuasion and let the Allies through. The Finnish government was unable to come to a decision either to accept the Russian terms or to make an appeal to the Allies. Only Paasikivi and M. Pekkala were unequivocally in favour of making peace, a substantial group of ministers was absolutely opposed unless the Russian conditions were moderated, and the rest hoped somehow to use the Allied offer of help to force the Russians to make concessions. At the end of a long debate all the government could agree upon was that Tanner must go back to Stockholm and exert moral pressure on Sweden to do something, or to agree to let the Allied expedition pass through.[25]

Tanner's remarks at the meeting of 25 February and his conduct in Stockholm, when he met Hansson on 27 February, support his claim that he too favoured making peace, but realized that the majority of his colleagues still had to be persuaded of the necessity. He certainly did ask Hansson for help in the form of substantial Swedish volunteer forces or, failing that, permission for the Allied expedition to pass through, but he was neither surprised nor distressed when Hansson replied that 16,000 was the maximum number of Swedish servicemen who could be released, and they must all be genuine individual volunteers. As for the Allied troops, 'no transit forces can be permitted. Volunteers and small groups might be permitted to pass through.' Hansson added that if the Allies tried to force a passage, they would be resisted and then 'Sweden would find itself in a war on the Russian side and against Finland.'[26]

It is a much-discussed question what Norway and Sweden would have done in reality if an Allied force had tried to cross their territory without permission. Officially they had to say that they would defend their neutrality,

[25] *Paasikivi*, pp. 152-7 : *Woodward*, p. 88 : *Tanner*, pp. 179-80.
[26] *Tanner*, pp. 181-5.

as they did in reply to the notes from Britain and France of 2 March asking for passage. But evidence published by the Germans after they had invaded Norway and captured the archives shows that the Norwegian government intended only token protest and resistance. It is equally improbable that Sweden would actually have engaged in hostilities with Allied troops once they had arrived; a more dangerous and realistic measure would have been to sabotage the railway. Ironside had written in his diary that 'to try to get up the Narvik railway without any help from the Swedish and Norwegian railway personnel is madness . . . We simply cannot do it.' Yet all that was needed was to cut off the electricity and the railway would be unusable, while the Swedish foreign minister, Guenther, told Tanner that they would not leave a single piece of track in place. So Norway and Sweden could have stopped the Allies without fighting them, but one may still doubt whether, in the event, and faced by the odium they would have incurred in the eyes of their own public by denying help to Finland in her hour of desperate need, they would have done so. Therefore the Swedish ministers felt that the only way to avoid disaster – and they foresaw correctly that the coming of Allied troops would be a disaster for everyone concerned – was to force the Finns to make peace first, on any available terms.[27]

So when Tanner went on to ask Hansson what Sweden could do to help if Finland did make peace, he at once got a positive response. Hansson confirmed that 'in his view peace should be made, even on hard terms', but that in that case Sweden was prepared to take up the idea of a Scandinavian defence alliance between Finland, Sweden and Norway to defend the new settlement, and could promise extensive economic aid for Finland's postwar reconstruction. This was what Tanner had really wanted – it was to be the sweetener that would persuade his colleagues to end the war on the Russian terms. The

[27] *Ironside*, p. 225: *Jakobson*, p. 245.

Finnish government met again on 28 February, and in addition to Tanner's report from Stockholm they had two new pieces of information. Firstly, the British ambassador had now delivered the true figures of the proposed Allied assistance; and secondly the Soviet government had sent a message through the Swedish government that Finland must give a definite reply to the Russian terms by eleven a.m. on 1 March. This forced a decision, and opinion in the government swung reluctantly behind Paasikivi and Tanner. Ryti led the waverers when he came out unambiguously for peace: 'We are compelled to seek peace even on the most onerous terms.' The war party clung on to one last straw: before a decision Mannerheim must give his opinion, and Ryti was sent with a deputation of ministers to consult the oracle. On the following day they returned to their colleagues with a depressing report. 'The Marshal's view of the situation was pessimistic. If the Russians achieved a breakthrough it would be difficult to hold them because of their masses of tanks. The ammunition situation was such that they were living from hand to mouth.' With this the opposition in the government collapsed, and the parliamentary parties, when they were consulted, agreed to accept the Russian terms. Late on 29 February the government debated the text of its reply, and despite some lingering opposition from two ministers, Hannula and Niukkanen, agreed to say that Finland 'accepted the terms in principle' and was willing to enter into discussion of the details in Moscow immediately.[28]

The Finnish government's decision to make peace was leaked to the Allied governments as soon as it had been made, and it triggered off among the Allied leadership a series of hysterical reactions, amounting in the end to a state of collective insanity. The French prime-minister, Daladier, was the first victim; his government had staked its existence on doing something to help Finland and in doing so turn the war into an anti-

[28] *Tanner*, pp. 183, 187: *Paasikivi*, pp. 160, 161.

communist crusade that would rally right-wing support in France, demonstrate that the Allies could take the initiative in the war, and divert the theatre of operations away from France. During the evening of 29 February, Daladier, without consulting his British ally, sent a message to the Finnish government which promised 50,000 men and 100 bombers to be in Finland by the end of March, with more to follow. The Allies would undertake to solve the problem of transit through Scandinavia. On the other hand, if Finland entered into negotiation with the Soviet Union, all Allied support would cease. This message was thoroughly dishonest, for there was no possibility of the promises being made good. The British cabinet was shocked when it learned of it and 'thought the French answers most disquieting. Their promises seemed to be bluff and to have been made in the knowledge that they could blame us for the failure to redeem them.' But instead of a firm repudiation of Daladier, the British ministers and their advisers gradually fell victim to the same hysterical compulsion to keep the Scandinavian project going at all costs. The cabinet succumbed first. Ironside noted on 2 March that they were seriously thinking of launching the expedition without the consent of Norway and Sweden, and Ironside, who was still rational at this point, remarked: 'The whole thing seemed rather nonsense to me.' For a time the caution of the professional advisers held the cabinet back. They insisted on telling Finland the truth about the size and timing of the expedition, and that it depended on the consent of Norway and Sweden, a position reiterated by the foreign office in face of French pressures as late as 6 March. This residual honesty of the British government lasted just long enough to save the Finns from calamity.[29]

Daladier's original message had achieved its effect: the Finnish government met on the morning of 1 March and all its members were taken in by the French offer. They were unanimous that it would be foolish to commit

[29] *Woodward*, p. 92: *Ironside*, p. 224.

themselves to accept Russia's terms until the Allied offer had been clarified. So the original message of acceptance was cancelled and a new one drafted which was intended to win time. It said that 'the Finnish government is anxious to bring about a cessation of hostilities and the conclusion of a peace, but since the new frontier contemplated in the proposal is vague, we request exact specifications and information what compensation Finland would get.' The Swedish foreign minister refused to forward this reply to Moscow unless a sentence was added stating that, even so, Finland accepted the terms in principle, and since the Finns would not agree to this, deadlock ensued. The Swedish government, desperate to keep the possibility of peace talks open, pursued unofficial soundings in Moscow to see if any clarification or modification of the Russian position was possible. The Finnish government used the time gained to press the Allies to confirm Daladier's offer, but because the British government would not lend itself to deliberate deception, they were told on 3 March that the first echelon would be of 12-13,000 men, that it would land in Norway on 20 March, but that the earliest date for any of these troops to reach Finland would be the middle of April. The figure of 50,000 was explained as being the establishment of the whole expeditionary force, and if Finland wanted this assistance she must make a formal appeal for Allied help by 5 March. The only immediate aid that the British could offer was fifty bombers, which would be flown in as soon as the appeal was received.

This reply settled matters for Tanner, who told the government on 3 March that they must now accept the Russian terms. He was supported by Paasikivi, who said that 'since the western powers' aid is not enough and will not arrive in time, and since, because of Sweden's attitude, it is uncertain and perhaps not possible, and since there is the further danger that we shall fall foul of Germany, we must get peace talks started and leave everything else aside.' Pekkala too supported Tanner, but although only Niukkanen and Hannula were in favour of sending a formal appeal for Allied help, the rest of the ministers insisted on waiting for some message from Moscow, in the belief that the threat of Allied intervention must make the Russans moderate their demands. But when on the morning of 5 March the government assembled again to face an unchanged situation, there had been no message from Moscow. There was, however, one from Mannerheim, which indicated that the situation around Viipuri was deteriorating and said that 'we must be prepared for unpleasant surprises. The western troops are insufficient and too late.' This message tipped the balance in the government and allowed it to come to a decision; with the exception of Hannula, the ministers agreed to forward to Moscow the acceptance which it had originally been intended to send on 1 March. Only if the Soviet government refused to talk would Finland turn to the western Allies, who were to be informed of the Finnish government's intentions. Tanner commented, and with justification, that the Finns had wasted the period from 1 to 5 March to no purpose, while both sides had incurred heavy additional casualties and the very possibility of peace had been put at risk by ignoring Moscow's deadline for acceptance. The responsibility lies not with the Finnish ministers, however, but with the French government, whose dishonest intervention had caused the delay.[30]

If the casualty figures are ignored, no great harm had been done, for that same day there came a message from the Soviet government to the Swedish government that the terms were still available. It was stated that if Finland delayed any further they would be hardened, because the Red Army was demanding to be allowed to advance further, and if necessary the Soviet Union could revert to dealing with the Kuusinen government. The Finnish reply was forwarded at once, together with a request for an immediate armistice, and the answer of the Soviet Government was in the hand of the Swedish government

[30] *Tanner*, pp. 203, 211-2: *Paasikivi*, pp. 167, 168, 169.

on the night of 5 March. It said that 'taking into account that the Finnish government accepts the terms, the Soviet government is ready to begin talks for the ending of hostilities and the establishment of peace.' But there could be no armistice before final agreement was reached, because the Russians did not trust the Finns and the Soviet terms would not be affected by the threat of Allied intervention. On 6 March the Finnish government chose the delegation that was to go to Moscow: it was led by Ryti, with Paasikivi as diplomatic adviser, General Walden to represent the military point of view and Professor Voionmaa, a member of the foreign affairs committee of parliament, to represent the politicians. The delegation left for Stockholm at once and arrived in Moscow on 7 March. They had no instructions from the government, and only one dubious bargaining-counter. When the Allied governments were told that Finland was going to enter into negotiations with Russia, they agreed to hold open their offer of assistance until 12 March – a date which would still allow the expedition to sail from British ports on the earliest planning deadline. So Finland still had a fall-back position, however unsatisfactory, if the negotiation failed, although nobody in the Finnish government, except Hannula, wanted to make use of it.

A review of the period since 29 January, when Russia first offered to make a negotiated settlement with the Finnish government, suggests that opportunities had been missed, and certainly shows how difficult it is to make peace while fighting continues and no military decision has been reached. It cannot be known at present what terms the Soviet government might have accepted before her military success on the isthmus, but it is plausible to guess that something like the October terms, without the compensation, might have been granted. Since this would have been much less onerous than the terms eventually imposed, it is easy to conclude that the Finns should have seized the opportunity – but this is not a realistic judgement. Until the front broke on the isthmus, the balance of military success was in Finland's favour. The performance of the Red Army had been pathetically inadequate, yet the Finns would have had to accept peace terms which, in effect, acknowledged defeat. Only some far-sighted, charismatic leader could have imposed acceptance on the Finnish people under these circumstances, and the only man who remotely met this specification, Mannerheim, was not then convinced of the necessity. It is sad but true that the great victories on the eastern front were in reality a positive curse for Finland: they could not change the ultimate outcome of the fighting, but they did make it psychologically impossible to conclude peace. Only the fact of defeat, and the death or mutilation of thousands of Finnish and Russian soldiers, could compel acceptance of what Paasikivi, almost alone among the Finnish leaders, saw to be inevitable.

When the Finnish government failed to make peace in early February, it had miscalculated the military and political possibilities of the situation, and again almost repeated this error in early March. It is to their great credit that on this occasion the Finnish leadership, with very few exceptions, assessed the worth of the Allied offer of assistance correctly. Although they were in a desperate position, and the Russian terms were hard, they found the courage to reject the proferred patronage and protection of two great powers. In part this is a reflection of how far Anglo-French policy had lost credibility since Munich; the recorded conversations of the Finnish leaders show that two names crop up again and again – Czechoslovakia and Poland. Finland's leaders had no wish to share the fate of these previous clients of Anglo-French protection. But, in addition, both the military and the civilian leadership saw through the Allied plans: they not only assessed the manifest inadequacy of the proposals, as soon as they got firm figures and dates, they also perceived that Finland's problems were being exploited by the Allies for other and ulterior ends. As Paasikivi wrote: 'We certainly understood in the government that the western powers had their own military purposes.' This good sense saved Finland from sharing in what the Norwegian campaign showed would have been a political and military disaster.[31]

Yet these same men, who so correctly assessed the worth of the Allied proposals, were as helpless as they had ever been in penetrating the intentions of the Russians. The delegation was sent off to Moscow in the confident expectation that there could be genuine negotiations as in October, with mutual bargaining and concessions. President Kallio said as much when he summed up the government's decision to send the delegation: 'I do not understand the situation to be that Peter the Great's frontier is to be adhered to without exception. The terms are a starting point for discussions, we are not obliged to consent to everything.' But the Finnish government now discovered, to its evident dismay, that this was precisely what it was required to do. The process of disillusionment began with the first meeting in Moscow on 8 March. The fact that Stalin did not take part in the talks meant in itself that there could be no real bargaining, for he alone on the Russian side had the power to make decisions. The Soviet delegation consisted of Molotov, Zhdanov and General Vassiljevski, and their job was to tell the Finnish delegation that it must accept the predetermined conditions unconditionally. Ryti had begun by appealing for a moderate settlement that could provide a firm basis for future good relations between the two countries. Molotov made an uncompromising response on the basis that Finland had been the willing tool of the imperialist and anti-Soviet policies of Britain and France. He said: 'We underestimated Finland's hostility. It has proved that Finland, as the weapon of other powers was more dangerous than we had believed. The war has proved this. *The Times* has written that the moment has come for an attack on the Soviet Union. This was openly and shamelessly said. You are the tool

[31] *Paasikivi*, p. 173.

of that policy. *Le Temps* wrote in the same fashion.' The
Finns naturally protested that they were not responsible
for what foreign newspapers chose to write, but Zhdanov
asked when the Finnish government had ever repudiated
such views or indicated that they would not allow Finland
to be used for such purposes. When the Finns insisted
that they had had no part in any Anglo-French designs,
Molotov made the grudging concession that 'your policy
may have been your own, but it was just the same as
the policy which the most aggressive circles in Britain
and France support.' From this Molotov argued that
Finland had no claim on the generosity of the Soviet
Union; she had proved unworthy of the consideration
that had been shown towards her in October.[32]

When Molotov read out the peace terms, the Finns
were dismayed to find that they included conditions
which had not been mentioned in the message passed on
by the Swedish government. The Soviet Union required that Finland should cede the whole of her part of
the Rybachiy peninsula, a strip of territory in the Salla-
Kuusamo area, where the eastern frontier came closest
to the Murmansk railway and that Finland should con-
struct a link line that would join the Murmansk railway
to the Swedish frontier at Tornio, on the Gulf of Bothnia. The Finnish delegates immediately protested at
what they considered to be the introduction of fresh demands, but Molotov insisted that they had all been
included in the terms transmitted to the Swedish government, except the Salla-Kuusamo demand, and in return
for this the Soviet Union was prepared to give back the
occupied Petsamo region to Finland. The discussions
were then suspended so that the Finns could study the
terms and consult with their government.

In Helsinki, Tanner was working hard to prevent his
colleagues going back on the policy they had chosen.
The military attaché in Paris, Colonel Paasonen, had
returned to Helsinki on 7 March, and he began lobbying vigorously for the acceptance of Allied assistance, so

[32] *Paasikivi*, pp. 172, 180, 181, 182.

Tanner hastily packed him off to headquarters at Mikkeli where he could do less damage. The next day it seemed that Tanner might have miscalculated, for Mannerheim had been talking to Paasonen, and he began to waver. Mannerheim telephoned Tanner and suggested that the government should appeal at once for Allied aid, without waiting for the outcome of the talks in Moscow, because 'the Russians are offering us impossible terms and the appeal might modify their demands.' Tanner refused to be swayed by this argument. He was convinced that 'the appeal would surely break off the negotiations in Moscow.' This was the background when the government met on 9 March and considered the report of the first meeting of its delegation with the Russians. They were disturbed and angry to learn that far from making concessions, the Soviet Union had added to the original demands. But the effect was offset by a report from the commander-in-chief on the military situation: Mannerheim had forwarded an assessment by General Heinrichs of the military prospects in the fighting on the isthmus. The report stated that 'the present state of the army is such that continued military operations can lead to nothing but further debilitation and fresh losses of territory'. Battalions were down to strengths of 250 men, weapons were being used up faster than they could be replaced, fighting efficiency was seeping away and at best the front might hold for a further week. On the basis of this report Tanner was able to persuade the ministers to authorize the delegation to accept the terms as reported. Tanner was able to relieve his own feelings by a telephone call to Guenther, in Stockholm, in which he protested that the Swedish government had apparently not been given the full Russian demands. Surely Sweden, as the mediating power, had some responsibilities in the matter. Guenther promised that Sweden would protest to the Soviet government at what appeared to be a deliberate deception, but when Tanner tried to press his advantage and asked 'can this development change the attitude of the Swedish government?'

he was told that 'that is difficult to answer, I do not believe so.'[33]

It is not clear whether the Soviet government had been guilty of deliberate misinformation in transmitting the terms, but it is true that as read out in Moscow they were not the same as those passed on by Stockholm. One difference was in Finland's favour, for Russia had dropped the demand for a mutual assistance pact – presumably the Russians could see that this would have been an empty mockery in the circumstances. The main novelty, the demand for the Salla-Kuusamo region, was always described by Molotov as a separate issue, a proffered exchange for the conquered Petsamo. On the other hand Molotov may have wanted to keep this demand from the Swedish government, because it was the one provision that might have been felt to be a direct threat to Sweden, and therefore it might have weakened the enthusiasm of the Swedish government for pressing Finland to settle.

The government sent a telegram to the delegation in Moscow which stated: 'Headquarters has furnished situation report: not sanguine about chances of carrying on . . . As continuation of war on the basis of aid promised is difficult and as contact with you is slow, we authorize you to decide the matter in all respects, provided you are unanimous.' When Mannerheim heard of the text he was dissatisfied, because he thought it failed to make the urgency of the military position clear to the delegation; at his insistence a second and more explicit telegram was despatched. But when the delegation met the Russians for the second time, on 10 March, they had not received either message, and tried to bargain for concessions on the grounds that the terms were not what Finland had been led to expect, and further put in a special plea that Finland should be allowed to keep the city of Viipuri. Molotov simply refused to discuss any modifications of substance, and hinted that if the Finns did not accept quickly there was always the Kuusinen

[33] *Tanner*, pp. 220, 222, 227, 228.

government to turn to. The tone of the exchanges is illustrated by what happened when Paasikivi pointed out that in 1721, when Peter the Great had established his frontier, he had paid a substantial monetary compensation. Molotov replied: 'Write a letter to Peter the Great, if he orders it then we will pay compensation.' The delegation then sent a telegram to Helsinki, saying that there was no prospect of winning any concessions, and asking for authority to settle.[34]

The Finnish government considered this message on the morning of 11 March, and the majority of the ministers agreed to submit to the inevitable, though with the most profound reluctance. President Kallio would have been willing to go on with the war if the government had been united, but only Hannula and Niukkanen were prepared to reject the Russian terms. These were then put to the foreign affairs committee of parliament, which voted for acceptance by thirteen to four. The delegation was told that 'the situation forces the government to accept the conditions.' When the two sides held their third meeting in Moscow, later on 11 March, it was possible for Ryti to announce that Finland had accepted the Russian terms, and he now tried to bargain for marginal modifications, but once more Molotov refused even to discuss most of his suggestions. He maintained a brutal and almost contemptuous attitude. When Ryti pointed out that Russia had not occupied all the territory that she was demanding, Molotov answered 'do you want us to take the areas in question first and then talk about them?' Ryti then said that surely the Finns were not to be sent away without the Soviet Union making any concessions at all, but Molotov retorted that 'any other great power in our position would demand war reparations, or all of Finland. If we continue the war there is no doubt we shall win.' The Finnish delegation then abandoned the argument and it was agreed to proceed to drafting the text of a treaty for immediate signature.[35]

[34] *Tanner*, pp. 230, 232: *Paasikivi*, pp. 184-5, 186.
[35] *Tanner*, p. 235: *Paasikivi*, pp. 187, 191.

As it became increasingly probable that Finland would make peace, and would not call on the Allies for help, desperation mounted in Paris and London, for peace would mean the end of their Scandinavian diversion and the whole plan to seize the initiative in the war with Germany. The French government put mounting pressure on the British to take some action which would induce Finland to issue the necessary appeal. Daladier insisted that his government could not survive politically if Finland went down to defeat without any Allied attempt to save her. The British government, which was politically more secure, yielded slowly to the mounting unreason of the French demands. The process through which the British succumbed can be seen in Ironside's diary. On 5 March he had agreed to lend his name to an attempt to deceive Mannerheim by a message describing the first echelon of the Allied expedition as 15,500 men, and implying that this number could be in Finland by the end of March – although Ironside knew this to be impossible. On 8 March he had wholly adopted the French view that it would be a major set-back for the whole Allied cause if Finland made peace. He wrote 'we are threatened with a defeat. How we are to escape from it I don't know.' In this mood, Ironside and the British leaders who accepted his advice were ready to grasp at anything that might revive the project, and the most promising way seemed to be to tell the Finns that the Allies would come to their help even if Norway and Sweden refused the right of passage, though Ironside had described this idea as nonsense as recently as 2 March. Some of the British cabinet, and in particular Lord Halifax and his foreign office advisors, who had always had grave reservations about the whole project, insisted as late as 10 March that the consent of the Scandinavian powers remained an essential pre-condition.[36]

On 11 March two developments occurred which helped to carry the British cabinet over the brink. The

[36] *Ironside*, p. 225; *Woodward*, pp. 95-7.

first involved a misreading of the intentions of the Finnish government. At its session on the morning of that day president Kallio had insisted that if they were to persuade Finnish domestic opinion of the necessity of accepting the Russian terms, they must be able to demonstrate that there was no practicable alternative. So it was decided to make an official approach to Norway and Sweden, and ask their governments openly whether they would permit the transit of an Allied expedition, or whether, if Finland made peace on Russia's terms, they would join Finland in a defensive alliance. The questions were submitted by Tanner by telephone and evoked the answers which he and most of the Finnish ministers had expected: the two governments would not permit transit but they would consider an alliance. The Finnish government was now in a position to tell the nation that peace had been made because Allied help was impossible, owing to the attitude of Norway and Sweden, and to console it with the prospect that, despite her losses, Finland would enjoy guarantees of security within her new frontiers. But the Allied leadership was led to assume that the Finnish request to Norway and Sweden meant that the Finns were wavering and that the issue of transit was the crucial one.[37]

The second development tied in with this. The French ambassador in London demanded that the British government agree to send the expedition without the consent of the Scandinavian powers, and he was supported by Ironside and Admiral Evans in the chiefs-of-staff committee, though Air Marshal Newall remained unconvinced, remarking 'I think the whole thing is harebrained.' The cabinet agreed that a public statement should be made, indicating the readiness of the Allies to proceed at once to Finland's rescue, and this was done later in the day by Chamberlain and Daladier in speeches to their respective parliaments. The operative clause in the British statement was that the two governments 'have

[37] *Tanner*, pp. 237-9.

already informed the Finnish government that they are
ready, at the request of the Finnish government, jointly
and without delay, to help Finland with all the means at
their disposal.' The Finnish ambassador was called to see
Chamberlain and told that the Allied help would be
unstinted, and that as an advance pledge twelve bombers
could fly to Finland at once, with forty-two more to
follow. The British cabinet now faced the final and
crucial test: if Finland responded to this offer, should
the expedition sail without the consent of Norway and
Sweden.[38]

Ironside had believed that the cabinet had already
resolved this question on 11 March, and that whatever
happened they meant to send the expeditionary force. He
was therefore shocked to discover on the morning of
12 March that the cabinet was still hesitating. He described them as 'a bewildered flock of sheep faced by a
problem they have consistently refused to consider . . .
I came away disgusted with them all.' By the afternoon
of 12 March the government had come to a decision,
though the form which it took reflected the agonies they
had gone through in making up their minds. First, the
original military conception was mutilated, since only
half of the projected operation was to take place initially:
the Narvik force, which could plausibly be represented
as intended to proceed to Finland, would sail but the
other half of the enterprise, the force which would secure
the southern Norwegian harbours, was to be held back
until German reactions provided the excuse for it. The
Narvik force would secure its base in the port, advance
up the railway into Sweden and concentrate there pre-
paratory to extending assistance to Finland. This looked
clear enough, but what followed was a commander's
nightmare of vagueness and contradiction. The orders
ran: 'It is the intention of his majesty's government that
your force should land, provided it can do so without
serious fighting . . . Fire upon Norwegian or Swedish

[38] *Woodward*, p. 97: *Ironside*, pp. 226-7: *Gripenberg*, pp. 139-40.

troops is only to be opened as a last resort. Subject to this you are given discretion to use such force as may be required to secure the safety of your command . . . It is not the intention of the government that the force should fight its way through Norway or Sweden . . . The decision as to the size of force to assist the Finns and the terms for its despatch is left to your discretion. It is important that the force to assist the Finns should be despatched as soon as possible.'[39]

On the surface these orders look like a sure recipe for catastrophe, since they scarcely make any coherent sense. The account of the meeting between the ministers and the force commanders, on the evening of 12 March does nothing to clarify them. Chamberlain himself interrogated the commanders about their understanding of the orders by putting a series of hypothetical questions to them. From these it appears that the force was expected to brush aside Norwegian resistance at Narvik, and then proceed to the Swedish frontier and demand passage. But if this was refused, the force would not attempt to force the frontier but would remain where it was. This looks so stupid that it is hard to credit that such orders were issued and accepted – and yet Ironside, a thoroughly professional soldier, was delighted by them: 'In the end all we wanted was passed . . . Thanks to Chamberlain we got things through.' In order to understand the thinking of the British ministers and service chiefs who subscribed to the issue of these instructions, it must be assumed that by this stage they had become so emotionally committed to the idea of a Scandinavian initiative as the means of breaking the deadlock in the phoney war that arguments against it were simply not given proper consideration. Even so, their calculations were not wholly unreasonable.[40]

The British leaders were least troubled by the aspect of their decisions that most bothers later commentators

[39] *Woodward*, p. 99: *Ironside*, pp. 227, 228: J. Kennedy, *The Business of War*, p. 49.
[40] *Woodward*, p. 99: *Ironside*, p. 227.

on their action – the way in which they incurred the danger of involvement in war with the Soviet Union. They simply did not rate this as a serious risk because the troops which eventually got to Finland would be technically volunteers in Finnish service, and there was no intention that Britain and France should declare war on Russia. On the other hand, when the cabinet considered the possibility on 12 March, they had so low an opinion of Russia's military potential that they decided that war with Russia was an unacceptable risk in view of the expected advantages to be won in Scandinavia. It is more difficult to understand why the Allied leaders were not deterred by the prospect that once the troops were ashore at Narvik, they would become trapped in the face of Scandinavian non-cooperation, since the orders are quite explicit that they might not use force to overcome this. So far as one can read the minds of the British and French ministers on this point, they were confident that once the troops were ashore, with the declared purpose of proceeding to the help of Finland, public opinion in Scandinavia would force the governments to let them through. Some of the military chiefs, like Ironside, had no worries on this score because they were sure that German reactions to the presence of Allied troops at Narvik would take care of all problems. The Allies would be able to forget about Scandinavian neutrality and helping Finland, and could get on with the real business of fighting the Germans. This was General Pownall's opinion when he wrote, on 13 March, 'of the four or five divisions that might have been sent across the North Sea not one division was intended for Finland – perhaps a brigade or two if they were lucky . . . The rest were simply for occupying and holding the iron-ore mines and for the support of Norway and Sweden . . . They weren't intended to go anywhere near Finland. It is really a most dishonest business.' It was indeed, but fortunately for the Finns and the world as a whole, the Allies failed in their attempts at deceiving Finland, just as they failed in every other branch of this lamentable enterprise, which Alan Brook aptly named 'the Finnish wild goose chase.'[41]

On the morning of 12 March the Finnish government met to consider a cable from the delegation in Moscow, which confirmed that there would be no concessions and asked for formal authority to sign the treaty. Niukkanen and Hannula alone took the position that it would be preferable to fight on and call for Allied assistance, and when it was clear that they had no support they offered their resignations. President Kallio agreed with them at heart. He was in evident distress at the role he was obliged to play, and declared that 'I shudder at these terms. I would be ready to go on with the war if I had support from the parliament and the cabinet, but gradually we have come to this pass.' As he signed the formal document, which gave the delegation powers to sign the treaty, he declared dramatically 'may the hand wither that is forced to sign such a paper as this.' Within a few months, his right arm was in fact paralysed by a stroke – but he had done his duty, and the authorization was transmitted to Moscow.[42]

The two delegations met there to approve the final text of the treaty, but Molotov cut short the proceedings with the blunt statement that no alteration to the text would be considered. Instead, he uttered a piece of barefaced effrontery when he said that 'I must point out that within our country, among extensive, very extensive military circles the idea prevails that Petsamo should not be returned to Finland. Although we never do anything that does not agree with the opinion of the nation, the Soviet government is prepared to leave the Petsamo area to Finland.' It is not recorded whether the Finns permitted themselves a smile at this version of how foreign policy is made in the Soviet Union. The Russians had in fact agreed to a few insignificant alterations to the text of the treaty in response to Finnish requests: they had increased the rent to be paid for Hanko, they had

41 *Pownall*, p. 290: A. Bryant, *The Turn of the Tide*, p. 75.
42 *Tanner*, pp. 244, 242.

FINLAND IN 1939
AND THE TREATY OF MOSCOW

Territory ceded by Finland
under Treaty of Moscow

Frontiers ·—·—·—
Railways ▪▪▪▪▪▪▪

added a mutual non-aggression clause, they had allowed more time for the completion of the railway to the Swedish frontier, and a few more days for evacuating the ceded areas. The treaty was signed in the early hours of the morning of 13 March and fighting ceased at twelve noon, Leningrad time, that same day.[43]

The treaty of Moscow is a brief document of nine articles and a protocol defining how it was to be executed. The purposes of the treaty are described as 'to create lasting peaceful relations' between Finland and the Soviet Union, and to ensure the 'security of the cities of Leningrad and Murmansk and of the Murmansk railway.' Finland ceded to the Soviet Union the islands in the Gulf of Finland, the whole of Karelia up to Peter the Great's frontier, including the towns of Viipuri, Käkisalmi and Sortavala, the Kuusamo-Salla area and Finland's part of the Rybachiy peninsula; in addition Finland granted a thirty-year lease of the Hanko peninsula and its adjacent islands as a naval base. The two powers were pledged to mutual non-aggression and neither was to enter into alliances directed against the other. Apart from the return of Petsamo to Finland, the remaining clauses were economic. The purpose of the railway to be built to the Swedish frontier was defined as the transit of goods between Russia and Sweden, and there was to be a trade agreement between Finland and the Soviet Union. The treaty was put before the Finnish parliament and approved on 15 March, and the ratifications exchanged in Moscow on 20 March. Formally, the Russo-Finnish war had ended.[44]

[43] *Paasikivi*, p. 193.
[44] There is an English text of the Treaty of Moscow in *Jakobson*, pp. 261-6.

V

The Consequences

The consequences of the Russo-Finnish war can best be analysed by examining first the effects it had on the two protagonists, and then the impact it had on the course of the Second World War. The Soviet Union had clearly been the victor in the conflict, and had dictated the terms of the peace, yet she had not realized all her aspirations and had paid a heavy price for her gains. Russia's initial war aim – the total conquest of Finland and the installation of a compliant puppet government – had not been achieved. This had been conceded on 29 January, when the Soviet government had agreed to enter into negotiations with the Finnish government in Helsinki. There had been subsequent occasions when Molotov had threatened to revive dealings with the Kuusinen government, but it had scarcely been a serious threat. Once peace was assured the Finnish Peoples' government announced that in the interests of avoiding further bloodshed it was disbanding itself and releasing the Soviet Union from its obligations. The acceptance of defeat on this point by the Soviet Union has proved to be final, but there is evidence that the policy had not been entirely abandoned at first. In April 1940, Kuusinen and his colleagues were installed as the government of a new Karelian-Finnish Soviet republic, which consisted of Russian Karelia with the addition of most of the areas ceded by Finland, and which was raised to the status of a full member republic of the Soviet Union. Zhdanov, in his speech at the inauguration of the republic, spoke of it as preparing the way for the brotherly comradeship of the Karelian and Finnish peoples: there seems little doubt that it was in the minds of the Soviet leadership that if ever an opportunity did present itself, the Karelian-Finnish Soviet republic, with Kuusinen at its head, could become the nucleus for a Soviet Finland. But, at most, the idea of an annexation of Finland was only an option, kept open for the Russian policy makers, and in the event no attempt was made to realize it. Even after 1944, when circumstances would have allowed the take-over of Finland by Russia, the attempt was not made: on the contrary, Kuusinen went back to Moscow for quite different tasks and the Karelian-Finnish Soviet republic was quietly downgraded and absorbed into the Russian Soviet Federated Socialist republic.

In effect, the Treaty of Moscow represented a reversion to a modified form of the original Russian policy of October 1939 – the extortion of concessions from Finland which would strengthen the defences of northern Russia against a possible great-power aggression. The new naval base at Hanko, with the islands in the Gulf of Finland, combined with Russia's positions in the Baltic republics gave her domination of the sea approaches to Leningrad. The territory in Karelia gave the possibility of organizing a defence in depth of the northern land approaches to Leningrad, the Salla-Kuusamo area placed strategic high ground covering the Murmansk railway in Russian hands and the sole possession of the Rybachiy peninsula greatly strengthened the possibility of defending Murmansk from an attack from the west. The one item in the treaty which cannot be accounted for in terms of obvious military advantage is the requirement to build the railway linking the Murmansk railway to the Swedish frontier. It has never been used for its declared purpose – the transit of goods between the Soviet Union and Sweden, and any other purpose it may have had remains a matter of speculation. The Finns believed at the time that it was intended to facilitate a swift Russian advance to cut Finland in two in a future war, and it could have served such a purpose;[1] or it could be the Russian reponse to the threat of an Anglo-French attack through Scandinavia (the Russians coming down

[1] E. Heinrichs, *Mannerheim Suomen kohtaloissa*, II, p. 199.

the new railway could hope to reach the Swedish frontier at about the same time as an Allied force coming through Narvik), all these, however, are simply guesses : the purpose of the railway remains an enigma.

From the Russian point of view the Treaty of Moscow provided a reasonable basis for the future relations of Finland and Russia; this seemed self-evident to the Soviet leaders, though they were a little surprised at their own moderation. Molotov was probably quite sincere when he told the Finnish delegates, after the signing, that 'the peace treaty just concluded is not a bad one, on the contrary it is in the interests of both parties, unless Finland clings to an alliance with the great powers. The Soviet Union is not afraid of Finland, but great powers can use Finland as a base for an attack on us. I am convinced that the treaty accords with the true interests of both countries, and I believe that in the future, on this basis, relations will be completely friendly.' He went on to assure them that Russia had no desire to interfere in Finland's internal affairs in the future. In the end, after some vicissitudes, events have largely borne out Molotov's predictions; the terms of the Treaty of Moscow have become the permanent basis for the relations of Finland and Russia, and these have become tolerably satisfactory for both parties. They were the basis for the settlement concluded after 1944, though on that occasion Finland lost Petsamo and had to pay war reparations, and Russian policy since 1940 has shown itself remarkably consistent. The Soviet Union has always reacted sharply when it has believed that any outside power was gaining influence in Finland, but provided that it has been confident that Finland is internationally isolated, and therefore ultimately in a situation of dependence on Russian benevolence, the Soviet government has been prepared to tolerate Finland's independence and her capitalist society within the framework established by the settlement of 1940.[2]

---

[2] *Paasikivi*, p. 196.

One reason why the Soviet Union gave up the idea of conquest in 1940 and did not pursue it after 1944, was because the war had shown that the military price of the conquest of Finland would be too high in relation to Russia's other military commitments. The war, which Meretskov affirms in his memoirs had been envisaged as a brief two to three week campaign had turned into a major military effort which had absorbed some 1,200,000 men, 1,500 tanks and 3,000 aircraft: Finland was just not worth that much sacrifice when the basic essentials could be secured by a treaty. As it was, the price which the Russians had paid had been a high one: official Soviet sources admitted to a loss of 48,000 killed and 158,000 wounded, but the Finns are convinced that the real figures should be much higher. Furthermore, in addition to the losses of men and material, the Red Army had exposed its weaknesses to the whole world and Russia was to pay a heavy price for this as well. In 1941, the gains made in the treaty did not compensate for these losses as Russia's defences were put to the test of war. Neither Hanko nor the new territory on the isthmus did much to protect Leningrad from the real danger, which came overland from the west and the south: Hanko was useless once the bases in the Baltic states were lost. Only in the far north, the one sector where the initial German attack on Russia did not succeed, did the sole possession of the Rybachiy peninsula and of the Salla-Kuusamo heights prove invaluable in blunting the German-Finnish thrusts against Murmansk and its railway.

But Russia did derive some military benefit from the war for it stimulated a movement of reform within the Red Army. The Military Supreme Soviet spent the period 14-17 April, 1940 evaluating the lessons of the Finnish campaign, and the results of the deliberation soon appeared. At the beginning of May Voroshilov was removed as commissar for defence and Timoshenko, the victor of the Finnish war, took his place. On 16 May a major new instruction for the Red Army, Order No. 120, was issued. It described the lessons of the war, listed

the shortcomings that had been exposed by it, and prescribed a massive programme of training and reorganiza-
tion to deal with them. Under Timoshenko's direction
commanders like Meretskov and M. Kirponov, who had
done well in the fighting, supervised extensive man-
oeuvres and realistic exercises. Parallel with this ran a
move back towards a more traditional type of military
professionalism. Former ranks and military discipline
were reintroduced into the Red Army and the process
culminated in the order of 12 August, 1940 reducing the
role of the political commissar in military units. The
principle of unitary command was re-introduced and
the professional officer was recognized as 'the sole leader
of the fighting forces'. There was not enough time in the
bare twelve months which followed May 1940 to enable
the Red Army to enjoy the full benefit of the reforms
dictated by its experiences in the war with Finland. But
when it was put to the test in 1941, against the best army
in the world, it performed just well enough to blunt, by
however narrow a margin, the initial German assault.
From the Russian point of view this was the military
profit to be set against the wastage of men and material
and the loss of prestige in Finland, and the near certainty
that if a foreign power did attack the Soviet Union, Finland would seize the opportunity to take her revenge –
as she did in 1941.[3]

For Finland, the defeated party in the war, the Treaty
of Moscow was a bitter blow, felt the more deeply because the general public was quite unprepared for such
drastic terms. The government, in order to keep up the
will to fight, had used its control of the press and radio
to create an impression that the military situation was
under control, and that there were real prospects of
valuable outside assistance. In consequence the news of
the peace terms, when they were released on 13 March,
was greeted with incredulous dismay, and the country
went into spontaneous mourning. It was the unfairness
that hurt the ordinary Finn most; they felt that they had

[3] *Meretskov*, p. 192: *Erikson*, pp. 553-5.

had a just cause, they knew that they had fought magnificently and yet in the end it seemed that wickedness and injustice had triumphed. It is a striking testimony to the basic soundness of Finnish society that it absorbed the shock unbroken – the nation as a whole yielded neither to despair nor recrimination, instead they made a virtue of the unity bred by the war and resolved to maintain it in the face of the new situation. In this they followed the lead given to them by such men as Mannerheim and Tanner, when they addressed the people at the end of the war. The speeches of the leaders claimed that the Finnish people had done all that was humanly possible in a just cause, that the whole world had admired their conduct and acknowledged their achievement, but that in the end Finland had been compelled to yield to overwhelming force. However, independence had been saved and the nation was still intact, and they could rebuild within their diminished homeland with the confidence which their achievements entitled them to feel. This line of argument seems to have been psychologically exactly right, for the Finnish people produced a remarkable response to the disaster which had struck them.

The most immediate problems caused by the peace were social and economic. The ceded areas contained nearly 450,000 people, or twelve per cent of the total population, and over half of them were small farmers. They had also contained the second city of Finland, Viipuri, about twelve per cent of the country's forest resources, seventeen per cent of the electrical generating capacity and fifteen per cent of the wood processing industry. Hanko had been Finland's principal winter harbour, seventeen per cent of the railway network had been lost and some of what remained was disrupted by the new frontier. On top of these losses were the losses incurred in the actual fighting. According to Finnish official figures, 25,000 men had been killed and 45,000 wounded, out of an army that had never had more than 200,000 men under arms. The material damages caused by enemy air activity had been comparatively superficial, but Finland had to carry the burden of debt for supplies and war materials obtained abroad on credit. Yet the Finns were extraordinarily undismayed by these problems. The most striking symptom of their will to recover was the almost unanimous decision of the population of the ceded areas to move into Finland. In the few days allowed before the Russians took over, a massive evacuation of property, farm-stock and other assets was carried through, so that the refugees should not be totally destitute. When the evacuation had been completed, the nation accepted a severe capital levy and stringent economic controls to enable the economy to be restored and the newcomers set up again in productive activity. This process was already well advanced when it was interrupted by war in June 1941, and was resumed after 1944. In the end Finland experienced a minor economic miracle. Since March 1940, Finland has fought and lost a second war, had Lapland devastated by her German ally, paid war reparations to the Soviet Union and successfully re-settled her refugees; and at the end of the process has emerged as, socially and economically, one of the most advanced and flourishing small European countries.

But the peace also left Finland with formidable problems in the fields of defence policy and foreign policy. From the military point of view the possibilities of defending the country successfully had been transformed very much for the worse. The new frontier was longer and more open than the old, and ran much closer to vital centres of population and industry. Finland could no longer afford in a future war to buy time for molibization by yielding territory in delaying actions before the main battle was joined. The first step was to build fortifications behind the new frontier and this was set in hand at once. Secondly, the army had to be reorganized so that it could give battle in shorter time and in greater initial strength. This too was done, the mobilization scheme was completely overhauled, the standing force of regulars and conscripts was considerably enlarged and by 1941 it was possible to mobilize the full sixteen-division army which Finland's population could support, so that in the second war Finland fielded 400,000 men. Further, this new and bigger army was much more nearly equipped to the standards required for contemporary warfare, and in branches like air defence and armoured forces and in supply of ammunition it was incomparably stronger. Thus the Finnish nation had given further proof of its vitality by assuming the burdens of civil reconstruction and extensive rearmament simultaneously.

The problems in foreign policy were not so easily or so satisfactorily solved. For the first months after the peace the situation was governed by the terms of the German-Soviet pact, and Germany still recognized that Finland belonged exclusively to the Russian sphere of influence. Then the German conquest of Norway virtually cut Finland off from direct contact with the west, and when followed by the military defeat of Britain and France, left her in a state of total isolation in her dealings with the Soviet Union. All Finland's efforts to diminish her dependence on Russia were frustrated: the hoped-for Scandinavian defence alliance, which was supposed to make the peace more acceptable, had been vetoed by Russia as soon as it was mentioned in public. Molotov told the Finns on 20 March that such an alliance would be regarded by Russia as an infringement of the peace treaty. In June 1940, when the Soviet Union finally annexed the Baltic republics, Finland was presented with a series of new demands. None of these was a matter of life and death for Finland, but cumulatively they were disturbing and sinister because they showed that Russia expected unquestioning compliance with all her wishes. The Finnish government gave way to some and resorted to delaying tactics on others. At the same time there was a resurgence of communist activity within the country: the Soviet government ostentatiously patronized this and alarmed the Finnish government further, because they interpreted it as an attempt at planned subversion – though they were in fact almost certainly mistaken about this.[4]

But these developments made it inevitable that when, in August 1940, Hitler ordered a change in German policy on Finland, with a view to using her in a possible attack on the Soviet Union, and secret approaches were made to the Finnish leaders which hinted at the possibility of German support against Russia, the Finnish leaders would seize the opportunity offered. From small and secret beginnings this Finnish-German collaboration developed to the point where, by June 1941, Finland had tacitly accepted her role in Hitler's 'Barbarossa' plan. She had agreed that in the event of a Russo-German conflict, which was still supposed to be purely hypothetical, Germany could use the territory of northern Finland to mount an attack on Murmansk. In addition, Finland had indicated that she would use any possible Russo-German conflict to regain her lost territories and would fight alongside Germany for this end. Thus Finland made the error, which is usually fatal for small powers, of backing the loser in a great power conflict. Yet the choice which Finland made in 1941, however mistaken it turned out to be, was an entirely natural one in view of the historical background and the recent course of Finnish-Russian relations, and it was equally natural that when, at the last moment, the Soviet leaders realized they had lost their grip on Finland, and tried to conciliate her and secure at least her non-intervention, the Finnish leaders did not respond. They had already staked their country's future on Germany proving victorious in any confrontation with the Soviet Union.

Although the Russo-Finnish war had remained a conflict formally separate from the greater European war, it has been shown how nearly the two wars became fused, bringing the Soviet Union in as an active co-belligerent of Germany. The Allies were only saved

[4] *Paasikivi*, II, p. 44.

from this ultimate folly by Finland's decision to make peace, bitterly though they regretted the decision at the time. The fact that in spite of the peace both the belligerent camps decided to pursue their Scandinavian plans means that, in the end, the Russo-Finnish war was the prime cause of the Norwegian campaign and all that followed from it. It also shows how Finland had been nothing more than a pretext for involving Scandinavia in the general European war; for when Finland dropped out of things both the Allied and the German leaders decided to pursue their plans regardless. It is true that the loss of the formal excuse caused a temporary pause on both sides, whose attitudes had become identical. Once the German leaders had committed themselves to 'Weserübung' they were as anxious as the Allies to have the chance of launching it. General Jodl shared the view of his opposite number, Ironside, when he noted in his diary on 10 March that the Finnish situation was 'disquieting, for if peace is concluded rapidly, it will be difficult to find a good reason for undertaking the operation.' This factor did indeed cause some delay in the German plans, for although the end of the war did not shake Hitler's determination to execute 'Weserübung', Jodl noted on 13 March that 'he is still looking for a reason for it.' The indecision did not last long, and by 26 March Hitler's mind was made up: 'Weserübung' was to go ahead. The operational orders for it were confirmed on 1 April, and the date for the seizure of Denmark and Norway was to be 9 April. Hitler's reason for proceeding was his confidence that, in spite of the ending of the Russo-Finnish war, the Allies would proceed with their plans in Scandinavia, and he was right.[5]

In the British camp, Ironside had been seeking, as had Hitler, for ways of keeping his Scandinavian project going. As he expressed it in his diary on 14 March, 'I have been thinking how I could keep alive the idea that we may be called upon to save Scandinavia.' Although

[5] *Trial of the Major War Criminals*, XXVIII, pp. 412, 413.

there was a minority among the Allied leaders who were
glad to have escaped from a project they had always
opposed, most of them shared Ironside's disappointment
at losing a chance to take the initiative. But the British
cabinet did not respond to Ironside's urgings, and decided that the expeditionary force should be dispersed.
The French reacted much more strongly to the set-back,
which did indeed, as Daladier had warned, cause the fall
of his government. But this meant that the new French
government under Reynaud was under pressure to
demonstrate its capacity to wage the war more effectively.
Therefore the French pressed vigorously for the revival
of the old British plan for laying mines in Norwegian
territorial waters, ostensibly to drive the ore ships out to
sea, but in reality with the deliberate intention of provoking a German reaction that would justify the execu-
tion of the plans for a new front in Scandinavia. This
policy became the decision of the Supreme War Council
on 28 March, and was confirmed by the British cabinet
on 1 April. The new plan, code-named 'Wilfred', involved tacking the Scandinavian expedition on to the
mine-laying plan, which was the necessary preliminary.
The whole of the original scheme was now reinstated so
that there would be two expeditionary forces, one which
would occupy Narvik, and a second that would take
Stavangar, Bergen and Trondheim. In this way the
Allies believed that they could seize the initiative in the
war and establish a Scandinavian front on terms favourable to themselves. They had, however, been forestalled:
by the time they had laid the first mines on 8 April, the
German forces were already on the move and it was the
Germans who landed first at Narvik on 9 April. Thus, in
the end, the only significant difference in the reaction of
both belligerent camps to the ending of the Russo-Finnish war was that Hitler made his mind up first and so
got his blow in before the Allies, thereby becoming the
formal aggressor. But as Lord Hankey, himself a member of the then British government, put it: 'If our operation was not an aggression, then their operation, which

was the only way of avoiding blockade, was not an aggression either . . . Everybody understood that the Germans were compelled to do it.'[6]

It was through the Norwegian campaign that the Russo-Finnish war made its immediate and demonstrable impact on the general course of the Second World War. But there was further influence which cannot be assessed with the same accuracy. This was the distortion in the calculations that world statesmen made about the balance of power, because they thought that the Red Army had been proved militarily incompetent and that Russia was therefore not really to be considered as a great power. This showed itself in the levity with which the Allied leaders had contemplated the chances of war with the Soviet Union in March 1940, and in the scepticism in Britain and the United States in 1941 about the value of the Soviet Union as an ally once she had been attacked. The idea that Russia would survive against Hitler for a few weeks or months at most, and that large scale assistance to her would be a misuse of resources, was deeply rooted. However, it was Hitler and the German planners whose actions were most deeply affected by this miscalculation. It cannot be said that Hitler would not have decided to attack the Soviet Union unless he had been blinded to the difficulties involved by his reading of the lessons of the Russo-Finnish war – he had other and weightier reasons for making his decision. But it did help to make the idea of the attack seem a practical proposition – it was possible for the Germans to plan in all seriousness to destroy the Red Army, and decide the war with Russia, in a single summer campaign. If any one event decided the defeat of Hitler, and hence the outcome of the Second World War, it was his decision to attack Russia in 1941. While it cannot be said that but for the apparent Russian fiasco in Finland, he would not have dared to take the risk of attacking the Soviet Union, it would be perverse to ignore the way in which the German interpretations of the lessons of the Russo-

[6] *Ironside*, p. 229.

Finnish war encouraged their leaders to make their most fatal error.

The Russo-Finnish war had become a popular myth over much of the world even before it had ended. Although it was soon consigned to oblivion beneath the impact of much greater events, at the time the attention of most of the world was focused on it. It seemed stupendous and portentous that a democratic nation of less than 4,000,000 people should defend itself with apparent success against a huge totalitarian tyranny. World reactions were not wholly spontaneous – naturally the professional anti-communists and Red-baiters made the most of the opportunity – but it remains true that millions of people in many countries felt uplifted by what they believed was happening before their eyes. After a decade in which might had mechanically triumphed over right, in which brute force alone seemed to rule the world, in which totalitarianism had monotonously trampled over democracy and freedom, Finland seemed to offer a contrary witness; at last right seemed to be winning over might against the most improbable odds. It looked like a nearly miraculous affirmation of the superiority of the human spirit over dark materialistic forces.

If this had been true it would have signified that the world is a better place than it is in reality – but it was not true. The Finnish people did indeed display courage, persistence against odds, self-sacrifice and devotion to a cause, in short all the qualities that are held to be most admirable in the human capacity for disinterested action. But if the human side of the Russian war-effort were as well known as the Finnish is, it must be suspected that the same splendid qualities displayed by the ordinary Finn in a good cause were equally to be found in his Russian opposite number in a bad one. Ultimately the Russo-Finnish conflict could only confirm the grim truth that war is a trial of brute force between the opposing parties and that in the end the side with the bigger battalions will win. Of course, force must not be reckoned crudely in terms of numbers of men and guns:

throughout history numerically inferior forces, helped by high morale and intelligent direction, have proved able to defeat enemies whose material strength was many times greater. But there is a limit to the extent to which morale and intelligence can compensate for material weakness, and by March 1940 Finland had reached that limit. There were no miracles in the Russo-Finnish war: all its various facets are capable of ordinary explanation when they are assessed coolly and dispassionately. Sadly the whole episode confirms that in a system of international relations based ultimately on the use, or threat of violence, the first question to be asked about the participants in any conflict is the one commonly ascribed to Stalin – how many divisions do they have? Finland had pitifully few, and it sealed her fate.

Yet the Finns feel to this day, and with reason, that their fate could have been worse. Other nations, some potentially much more powerful than Finland, suffered much more – it is only necessary to consider the misfortunes of Poland, a comparison the Finns themselves are fond of making. But this does not mean that Finland and her people possess some mysterious special qualities which other peoples lack. Finland did have certain advantages: for instance the strength which a liberal democratic society can generate, as well as its weaknesses; a population which, in spite of its deep internal divisions, had an overriding sense of its separateness and common identity against all outsiders, of its possession of a territory uniquely its own, which all were prepared to fight for if they must. Further, although Finland had neglected to prepare its defences to the maximum extent that would have been possible, enough intelligent thought and preparation had been devoted to problems of defence to make the Finnish armed forces exceptionally effective in relation to their size. But these things by themselves could not have saved Finland. They needed to be combined with the historical chance which had settled the Finnish people in their peculiar geographical situation. It was shown at the outset of this work how Finland did have various kinds of strategic significance for outside powers; but in the overall geopolitical structure of Europe, Finland's significance is marginal, her strategic possibilities interesting but not crucial – there was for instance nothing in Finland equivalent to the strategic significance of the Swedish iron-ore fields. And because Finland was of marginal importance, because she was and is located aside from the great strategic axes along which the European power struggle flows, it was not worth the effort needed to smash her relatively formidable powers of resistance and take the country over. This combination saved Finland. The fact that she was able to put up an effective defence together with the fact that she was not of first-rate strategic significance preserved Finland, when so many other small nations went down to disaster. It is because of this that the myths of the Russo-Finnish war could be dangerous. Nations may come to believe that will and morale can compensate for material weakness and ensure survival in a world based on power politics. This is simply not true and the Russo-Finnish war shows it. There can be no security for the small and the weak, however heroic they may be, as long as the relations between states are based on the ultimate sanction of war.

BIBLIOGRAPHY

Original materials for the history of the Russo-Finnish war are fairly abundant, but unevenly distributed. The archives of the British government are now open, and Woodward's official history, *British Foreign Policy in the Second World War*, is a useful introductory guide. The surviving German government records are also freely available and *Documents on German Foreign Policy* give a good selection from the Foreign Ministry papers. The position over Finnish government records is obscure; foreigners at least do not have free access to them. The *Finnish Blue-White Book* has a selection of documents but it is understandably slanted in Finland's favour. Important private archives, notably those of Paasikivi and Mannerheim, are still closed to research, but Paasikivi's memoirs give a generous selection of minutes of his talks with the Russian leaders, extracts from his personal diary and notes of sessions of the Finnish government. Tanner's memoirs also contain the texts of many official and private documents of importance. The great gap in the availability of original sources is caused by the fact that the Russian archives remain firmly closed, and since on the whole the régime would like to forget about the Russo-Finnish war, it seems unlikely that much material will be forthcoming. The most accessible Soviet version is in the official history of the Great Patriotic War. There is a large secondary literature in English, though the flood of publications written during and immediately after the war is nearly all superficial journalism or propaganda produced by writers whose real knowledge of either Finland or Soviet Russia was minimal. The best English-language account of the politics and diplomacy is in Jakobson; and of the military operations, in Mannerheim's memoirs. The literature in the Finnish language is by now extensive, for there was a flood of writings in the immediate aftermath, though since 1945 this has dried up – perhaps it is felt to be unneighbourly now to dwell on it too much. The following bibliography is therefore only a small selection of what it is hoped are the more useful and significant publications.

Finland 1939-1940

Documents and official sources

Documents on German Foreign Policy, Series D (1937-41), VIII, London, HMSO, 1954.

Handlingar rörande Sveriges politik under andra världskriget: Forspelet till det tyske angreppet på Danemark och Norge den 9 April 1940, Stockholm, Swedish government publication, 1947.

LEHMUS, K.: *Talonpoika suurten shakkilaudalla: Talvisodan dokumentteja*, Helsinki, Weilin & Göös, 1969.

SEPPALA, R.: *Mainilan laukaukset: muistelmia ja muistiinpanoja tapahtumista Karjalan kannaksella syksyllä 1939*, Tampere, Tampereen Kirjapaino-osakeyhtiö, 1969.

Soviet Documents on Foreign Policy 1917-1941, Oxford, OUP, 1953.

The Development of Finnish-Soviet Relations (The Finnish Blue-White Book), Helsinki, Finnish government publication, 1940.

Trial of the major War Criminals, XXVIII, Nuremburg, 1948.

Books and published works

BOND, B. (Ed.): *Chief of Staff: The Diaries of Lieutenant General Sir Henry Pownall*, I, 1933-1940, London, Leo Cooper, 1972.

BRYANT, A.: *The Turn of the Tide*, London, Collins, 1957.

BUTLER, J. R. M.: *Grand Strategy*, II, London, HMSO, 1957.

CHURCHILL, W. S.: *The Second World War, I, The Gathering Storm*, London, Cassell, 1948.

CLARK, D.: *Three Days to Catastrophe*, London, Hammond, Hammond & Co., 1966.

DERRY, T. K.: *The Campaign in Norway*, London, HMSO, 1952.

ERIKSON, J.: *The Soviet High Command: a military political history 1918-1941*, London, Macmillan, 1962.

FEILING, K.: *Life of Neville Chamberlain*, London, Macmillan, 1946.

Bibliography

GAMELIN, M.: *Servir*, Paris, Librairie Plon, 1947.

GRIPENBERG, G. A.: *Finland and the Great Powers: Memoirs of a Diplomat*, Lincoln, Nebraska, University of Nebraska Press, 1965.

HALSTI, W. H.: *Suomen sota 1939-1945*, I, *Talvisota*, Helsinki, Otava, 1956.

HEINRICHS, E.: *Mannerheim Suomen kohtaloissa*, Helsinki, Otava, 1959

Istoriya Velikoi Otechestvennoi Voiny Sovestskogo Soyuza 1941-1945, I, Moscow, 1960.

JAKOBSON, M.: *The Diplomacy of the Winter War*, Cambridge, Mass., Harvard University Press, 1961.

KENNEDY, J.: *The Business of War*, London, Hutchinson, 1957.

KIVIMAKI, M. T.: *Suomalaisen poliitikon muistelmat*, Porvoo, Werner Söderström, 1965.

KORHONEN, K.: *Suomi neuvostodiplomatiassa Tartosta talvisotaan*, II, 1933-39, Helsinki, Tammi, 1971.

LINKOMIES, E.: *Vaikea aika*, Helsinki, Otava, 1970.

LUNDIN, C. L.: *Finland in the Second World War*, Bloomington, Indiana University Press, 1957.

MANNERHEIM, C. G., *The Memoirs of Marshal Mannerheim*, London, Cassell, 1953.

Muistelmat, Helsinki, Otava, 1952.

MERETSKOV, K. A.: *Na sluzhbe naroda*, Moscow, 1968.

MACLEOD, R., and KELLY, D. (Eds.): *The Ironside Diaries 1937-1940*, London, Constable, 1962.

Nazi-Soviet Relations 1939-1941, Washington, U.S. Department of State, 1948.

NEVAKIVI, J.: *Apu jota ei pyydetty*, Helsinki, Tammi, 1973.

NIUKKANEN, J.: *Talvisodan puolustusministeri kertoo*, Porvoo, Werner Söderström, 1951.

PAASIKIVI, J. K.: *Toimintani Moskovassa ja Suomessa 1939-1941*, Porvoo, Werner Söderström, 1959.

TANNER, V.: *The Winter War*, Stanford, Stanford University Press, 1957.

TUOMINEN, A.: *Kremlin kellot: muistelmia vuosilta 1933-1939*, Helsinki, Tammi, 1957.

Myrskyn aika, Helsinki, Tammi, 1970.

VON BLUCHER, W.: *Gesandter zwischen Diktatur und Demokratie*, Wiesbaden, Limes Verlag, 1951.

WIGFORSS, E.: *Minnen*, III, 1932-1949, Stockholm, Tidens Förlag, 1954.

WOODWARD, L.: *British Foreign Policy in the Second World War*, I, London, HMSO, 1970.

INDEX

Index

171

Index

Leningrad, 13, 14, 17, 21, 28, 29, 31, 34, 44, 45, 47, 48, 49, 95, 96, 107, 148, 150; security of, 14, 17, 22, 23, 29, 32, 47, 49
Litvinov, M., 18, 19
Luleå, 99, 101

Mainila incident, 47, 49, 63
Mannerheim, G., 21, 33, 35, 36, 43, 50, 62, 65, 66, 67, 70, 72, 87, 88, 89, 96, 98, 105, 113, 114, 115, 117, 130, 133, 138, 139, 141, 154
Mannerheim line, see Karelian isthmus
Meretskov, K., 22, 23, 49, 57, 63, 64, 107, 108, 152, 153
Mikkeli, 62, 138
Molotov, V., 21, 28, 29, 30, 35, 36, 40, 44, 47, 48, 76, 92, 93, 96, 97, 108, 136, 137, 139, 140, 146, 149, 151, 156; speech of (31.10.39), 38-40; (30.11.39), 49-50
Moscow, 12, 18, 20, 24, 26, 35, 38, 43, 49, 92, 93, 96, 126, 130, 132, 133, 134, 136, 138, 139, 140, 146, 148; treaty of, 140, 146-8, 150-51, 153, 155; consequences of for Finland, 154-5
Murmansk, 13, 29, 63, 148, 150, 152, 157
Murmansk railway, 13, 63, 137, 148, 150, 152

Narvik, 99, 101, 103, 129, 143, 144, 145, 151, 159
Naval forces (British), 12, 29; (Finnish), 53; (German) 29
Niukkanen, J., 32, 33, 36, 38, 106, 130, 133, 140, 146
Norway, 13, 16, 21, 79-81, 95, 96, 99, 100, 101, 103-5, 125, 127-9, 131, 132, 141-4, 156, 158

Oesch, K., 31, 115, 122
Öhqvist, H., 31, 61, 111, 113, 114, 117, 122
Österman, H., 31, 61, 62, 113

Oulu, 62, 66, 67

Paasikivi, J., 26, 29, 30, 32, 34, 38, 40, 43, 48, 50, 71, 72, 73, 77, 91, 92, 93, 96, 105, 106, 126, 128, 130, 132, 134, 135, 140
Petsamo, 13, 63, 67, 80, 98, 102, 103, 104, 137, 139, 146, 148, 151; nickel deposits in, 13
Poland, 24, 27, 39, 42, 98, 135, 162

Relander, H., 12
Ribbentrop, J. von, 26, 78, 125
Russia (Soviet Union, USSR):
    and the Allies, 18, 22, 23, 96, 136, 137, 150; and Finland, 11, 12, 14-8, 20-3, 31, 32, 35, 36, 39, 40, 42, 44, 47, 49, 50, 73, 74, 76, 92-5, 97, 134, 136-40, 146, 148-53, 156, 157; and Germany, 22, 24, 29, 30, 93, 98; and Great Britain, 15, 18, 22, 29, 30, 136; leaders of, 15, 21, 28, 39, 40, 93, 94, 108, 149, 151, 157; October revolution in, 11; purges in, 45, 58, 75; Tsarist regime in, 11
Russian (Red) army, 17, 30, 47, 48, 56-61, 63-70, 83, 84, 86-91, 95, 98, 107-12, 114-17, 119, 120, 130, 133, 135, 152, 157, 160; equipment of, 56, 152; mobilization of, 56, 58; operational plans of, 22-3, 60, 63, 64, 68, 116, 117, 120; training and tactics of, 57-9, 83, 86, 87, 89, 91, 107, 108, 110, 115, 117, 153
Russian government, 11, 19, 28, 48, 95, 130, 133, 138, 139, 146; its Finnish policies, 22, 23, 44-6, 49, 73, 75, 94-5, 107, 108, 149-50
Russo-Finnish negotiations 14, 16; (1938), 19-20; (1939), 14, 21, 26-30, 34-5, 36, 40-2; (1940), 92-4, 96-7, 107, 114, 123, 126, 128, 130-42, 146, 148

173